Robert Morris

Masonic Odes And Poems

Robert Morris

Masonic Odes And Poems

ISBN/EAN: 9783744714440

Printed in Europe, USA, Canada, Australia, Japan

Cover: Foto ©Thomas Meinert / pixelio.de

More available books at **www.hansebooks.com**

MASONIC

Odes and Poems.

By ROB MORRIS, LL. D.,

MASONIC WRITER.

> Thus life and beauty come to view,
> In EACH DESIGN our fathers drew,
> So glorious and sublime;
> EACH breathes an odor from the bloom
> Of gardens bright beyond the tomb,
> Beyond the flight of time.

New York:
ROB MORRIS, NO. 545 BROADWAY;
MACOY & SICKELS, 430 BROOME ST.
1864.

BAKER & GODWIN, Printers,
Printing-House Square, opposite City Hall,
New York.

TO

GEORGE OLIVER, D. D.,

OF SCOPWICK VICARAGE, ENGLAND.

YOUR RESEARCHES IN THE

History and Spirit of Masonic Symbolisms

Have awakened new interest and inaugurated a

BETTER ERA IN THE LITERATURE

OF THE BELOVED

ART.

THE LAMENTED SCOTT, OF MISSISSIPPI,

Was one of the sons of your genius, and an entire generation of Masonic writers has acknowledged your preëminence.

PERMIT ONE OF THE HUMBLEST OF THE FAMILY TO
LAY AT YOUR FEET THIS VOTIVE WREATH,
AND TO ASK ITS ACCEPTANCE.

PREFACE.

SOME of these pieces have gone the rounds of the press, masonic and secular, for a considerable period, and have attracted the favorable attention of the public. Others have been examined in manuscript by persons whose judgment in matters of this kind is admittedly worthy of consideration. The author has recited many of them in discourses to lodges and public assemblies. These authorities seem to concur in a verdict, and to express the wish that the pieces, as a whole, may be published.

Whatever predilection the author may feel for his literary offspring, he would not have ventured upon so daring an experiment as a volume of Masonic poems but for these assurances of favor; and if, after all, he has misunderstood the general expression upon this subject, he casts himself upon the forbearance of those whose good opinion he has so long sought to propitiate.

NEW YORK, JUNE, 1864.

CONTENTS.

	PAGE
The Sowing of the Seed	13
Setting a Memorial	15
The Level and the Square	17
The Goodly Heritage	19
Yearnings	20
King Solomon's Farewell	21
Quarry, Hill, and Temple	24
Fragrance of a Good Deed	26
A Parting Hymn	27
Song for St. John's Day	28
The Obedient Disciple	29
Via Lucis, Via Crucis	31
The Beacon-Light	32
Voice of the Temple	33
Building the Fane	33
Hymn of the Mason-Soldiers	35
Earnestness of Covenanting	36

	PAGE.
The Fervor of Affiliation	37
The Enclosure	38
Masonic Training	39
Ask! Seek!! Knock!!!	40
Masonic Auld-Lang-Syne	41
Tears and Smiles	42
Nunc Dimittis	43
Lingering Notes	45
The Giving of the Shoe	46
Inscriptions for a Lodge-Room	47
The Pillars of the Porch	48
Cherishing the Pledge	49
Let Your Light Shine	50
Brotherly Love	51
The Fire of Friendship	52
Words of Peace and Love	53
The Pilgrim's Home	54
Hymn for Consecration	56
The White-aproned Brothers	57
Hours of Praise	59
The Dying Hope	61
Ono	62
Pledge to a Dying Brother	63
A Look to the Orient	65
Prayer—Oral or Secret	66

PAGE.

The Song of St. John............................ 67

Tribute to Washington........................ 69

The Broken Column............................. 70

A Mason's Epitaph.............................. 71

Death, the Celestial Gate...................... 72

Burns' Farewell................................ 74

The Crescent................................... 75

Duties of the Craft............................ 76

Verdant, Fragrant, Enduring 77

Fredstole: the Seat of Peace 78

Ode for a Winter Festival...................... 79

The Quarry of Life............................. 80

The Cedar Tree................................. 81

A Lodge Valedictory 82

Hard Service, Good Wages....................... 83

Faith of the Olden Time....... 85

The Resurrection............................... 87

Consecration of a Cemetery..................... 88

So Mote it Be.................................. 90

A Hebrew Chant................................. 91

Go on thy Bright Career 92

The Freemasons' Home 93

The Dying Request.............................. 94

The All-Seeing Eye............................. 96

Appreciation................................... 97

PAGE.

Leaning Towards Each Other. 98

The Hour of Eleven............ 100

Corn. Wine. Oil 102

Tribute to Robert Burns.............................. 104

The Foundation Stone.... 105

The Inheritance of Friendship......................... 106

To Masons Everywhere..... 108

A Masonic Greeting 110

The Happy Hour....................................... 111

The World-wide Recognition........................... 112

The Widow and the Fatherless......................... 113

The Death of the Grand Master....................... 115

The Veteran's Lament 117

Washington 119

The Three Salutes... 124

The Master of the Upright Heart...................... 125

Masonic Valedictory.................................. 128

A Masonic Symposium................................. 130

The Narrow Boundary................................. 132

New Year's Reflections................................ 133

Timely Warning 135

A Welcome into Masonry.............................. 136

Dividing the Tessera....... 138

High XII... 140

The Checkered Pavement.............................. 141

PAGE.

The Focus of the Lodge 143

The Decayed Lodge................................... 144

The Duelist... 146

The Tracing-Board.................................. 147

Fellow Crafts' Song................................. 149

The Teacher to His Pupils........................... 150

Tribute to a Friend................................. 152

The Two Visits..................................... 153

Brother's Last Request.............................. 155

A Festival Ode 156

Centennial Ode..................................... 158

Grave of the Grand Master 159

Rise Up: He Calleth Thee............................ 161

The Dark Decree.................................... 162

The Pursuit of Franklin 163

Monody to the Hon. P. C. Tucker...................... 166

Song and Freemasonry.............................. 167

The Funeral Sound.................................. 169

Crypt in the Corner-Stone........................... 170

Our Future Meeting................................. 171

Emblems of the Craft............................... 172

Solomon's Midnight Visit 174

The Spirit of Union................................. 176

The Orient 178

The Passage of Time................................ 179

PAGE.

The Model Mason.................................... 180

The Loving Tie....................................... 181

The Hour Glass....................................... 183

The Cheerful Hour at High XII. 184

Knight Templar's Dirge............................... 185

The Test... 186

A Dedication... 188

Lines to Lexington Lodge............................. 189

Walking Together..................................... 190

Exhortation to Charity............................... 191

The Temple 192

The Wise Choice of Solomon.......................... 195

The Celestial Record................................. 197

The Perfect Ashlars.................................. 198

The Last, Last Word 199

MASONIC ODES AND POEMS.

The Sowing of the Seed.

We are exhorted, in that Volume about which an OBLONG SQUARE is formed in a Masonic Lodge, "to sow beside all waters." In a lodge of Freemasons, no more than in any other society, is there perfect sameness in sentiment and choice. While similarity in physical, mental, and moral qualifications is needful in the construction of our social edifice, there are diversities of character sufficiently marked among us to justify the poet in offering the following paraphrase of Luke viii. 5–8, as his Salutatory:

He that hath ears to hear,
    May listen now,
While I shall tell, in mystic words indeed,
Of a good husbandman who took his seed
    And went to sow.

Some by the wayside fell;
    On breezes borne,
The fowls of air flew down, a greedy train,
And snatched with hasty appetite the grain,
    Till all was gone.

Some fell upon a rock ;
And greenly soon,
They sprouted as for harvest, strong and fair ;
But when the summer sun shone hotly there,
They wilted down.

Some fell among the thorns—
A fertile soil—
But ere the grain could raise its timid head,
Luxuriantly the accursed plants o'erspread,
And choked them all.

But some in the good ground—
God's precious mould—
Where sun, breeze, dew, and showers apportioned well ;
And in the harvest, smiling swains could tell
THEIR HUNDRED FOLD !

Following the ancient example, we would disseminate the thoughts with which we are charged in every part of the mystic work, in quarry, hill, and temple ; among the tall cedars ; upon the floats ; upon the road from Joppa to Jerusalem ; in the crypts of the Holy Mountain,— wherever, for moral and sacred purposes, the MASTER wields his Gavel or the WORKMEN prepare sound blocks and set them duly in place.

Setting a Memorial.

A MEMORIAL is that which preserves the memory of a person, place, or event. In olden times, a pillar, a heap of stones, or a mound was raised by contracting parties to perpetuate friendships. The ancient landmarks of Masonry, morally considered, are MEMORIALS of the boundary lines set up by the Royal Originator of the great Institution.

The objects most appropriate for MEMORIALS between Masons, are the TESSERA (of which something will be said hereafter) and the EVERGREEN SPRIG, the subject of the present lines. The latter is more emblematical than the former, as referring more directly to events that formed part of the Initiatory services of Masonry, and were indelibly engraven upon the candidate's heart. The EVERGREEN SPRIG represents the SPRIG OF ACACIA, an oriental plant with oriental allusions explained best in the esoteric traditions of Masonry

The instructed mind fastens upon this emblem. It is equally grateful in *fragrance* as in *verdure*, and it long resists the power of decay. The lessons it imparts, as it falls from the brotherly hand into the open grave, are full of pathos and solemnity. For ages it has been wet with the tears of mourners as it mingled with the fresh sods of mother-earth upon the coffin of the departed friend, until it seems, to the fanciful ear, to whisper from its native bough the song of faith undying, and of perfect love.

We'll set a green sprig here to-night,
    To rescue, from the days to come,
Each bright and joyous memory,
    That henceforth gilds this festive room ;
And should occasion e'er require
    A token, to recall the place,
THESE LEAVES will bring to clearest view,
    The cheerful thought and sunny face.

We'll set a green and deathless sprig—
  Each leaf a BROTHER's NAME shall have;
And fragrant will th' Acacia bloom
  When one has parted to the grave:
When one in Temple-labors fails,
  And golden bowl is broken quite,
How grateful to the sense will be
  The green sprig that we set to-night!

We'll set the sprig with every hand—
  Come round, and plant the deathless tree!
There is not one in all this band,
  But what is marked by destiny;
Death comes to all—how well to know
  There is a life beyond this scene,
Whose deathless limit may be read,
  Oh Brothers, in this sacred green!

We'll set the green sprig deep in love;
  We'll water it with sympathy;
We'll give it fond and faithful care,
  Nor shall a single leaflet die;
And when the last of this true band,
  Death's mighty puissance shall attest,
May those who follow after say,
    FAITHFUL AND TRUE, HOW SWEET THEY REST!

The Level and the Square.

These lines, written in the summer of 1854, have acquired a popularity equaled, perhaps, by no similar production, since the "Farewell" of Robert Burns, whose pathetic words:

> "Adieu! a heart-warm fond adieu,
> Dear brothers of the mystic tie,"

have opened the fountain of tears in three generations of Freemasons. Set to no less than ten distinct melodies, several of them original, and of rare merit, "The Level and the Square" is sung at LABOR and at REFRESHMENT, upon the journey, at the grave's side, in the domestic circle, and wherever else Freemasons congregate to do Masons' work or to enjoy Masons' wages.

The writer is not so presumptuous as to attribute this great favor to the merit of the lines themselves, but rather to the theory which they present of the relation which the EARTHLY bears to the HEAVENLY LODGE. This theory accords with the general view entertained of Masonry through all the historic period, at least.

We meet UPON THE LEVEL and we part UPON THE SQUARE;
What words of precious meaning those words Masonic are!
Come, let us contemplate them, they are worthy of a thought—
In the very soul of Masonry those precious words are wrought.

We meet UPON THE LEVEL, though from every station come—
The rich man from his mansion, and the poor man from his
　　home;
For the one must leave his heritage outside the Mason's door,
While the other finds his best respect upon the CHECKERED
　　FLOOR.

We part UPON THE SQUARE, for the world must have its due;
We mingle with the multitude, a faithful band and true;
But the influence of our gatherings in memory is green,
And we long UPON THE LEVEL to renew the happy scene.

There's a World where all are equal, we are hurrying towards it
    fast;
We shall meet UPON THE LEVEL there, when the gates of death
    are past;
We shall stand before the ORIENT, and OUR MASTER will be there
To try the blocks we offer WITH HIS OWN UNERRING SQUARE.

We shall meet UPON THE LEVEL there, but never thence depart;
There's a MANSION—'tis all ready for each trusting, faithful
    heart—
There's a MANSION and a WELCOME, and a multitude is there,
Who have met UPON THE LEVEL and been tried UPON THE
    SQUARE.

Let us meet UPON THE LEVEL then, while laboring patient here;
Let us meet and let us labor, though the labor be severe;
Already in the WESTERN SKY the signs bid us prepare
To gather up our WORKING TOOLS, and part UPON THE SQUARE!

Hands round, ye faithful Masons, in the bright, FRATERNAL
    CHAIN!
We part UPON THE SQUARE below, to meet in HEAVEN again;
Oh! what words of precious meaning those words Masonic are,
We meet UPON THE LEVEL and we part UPON THE SQUARE!

The Goodly Heritage.

The Psalmist, expressing the hope of his calling, of the resurrection, and of life everlasting, cries aloud, in an ecstacy of gratitude, " The lines have fallen unto me in pleasant places; yea, I have A GOODLY HERITAGE;" and afterwards, in recounting his former experience, he confesses that God has heard his vows and has given him the HERITAGE of those that fear His name.

Oh what a goodly heritage
    THE LORD to us hath given !
How blest the brotherhood that pledge
    Their Mason-vows to heaven !
We sing the mystic-chain that binds
    These western realms in one;
Such loving hearts, such liberal minds,
    No other land has known.

Five thousand lights in Mason-halls,
    Are gleaming on our eyes;
Five thousand emblems on the walls,
    Tell whence the gleaming is;
And when the portals ope, to pass
    The humble seeker in,
THE VOICE OF PRAYER pervades the place,
    And proves the light DIVINE !

On every hill our brothers lie,
    And green sprigs deck the knoll;
Their fall brought sorrow to the eye,
    But triumph to the soul:

Our orphans lighten many a home,
  Our widows' hearts are glad,
And Mason-light dispels the gloom
  And comfort finds the sad.

Thus link in link, from shore to shore,
  The mystic chain is wound;
Oh, blended thus forever more,
  Be Mason-spirits found!
And while the heavens, on pillars sure,
  Of STRENGTH and WISDOM stand,
May brotherhood like ours endure,
  Where Strength and Wisdom blend!

Yearnings.

Brothers, when o'er my head,
  The silent dust is spread,
And this poor heart its quiverings shall forbear,
  Where'er my body lie,
  Though far the grave away,
I would, dear Brothers, be remembered *here!*

Brothers, when tender sighs
  Around me shall arise,
And speak of what I did, or fain would do,
  Such honest, truthful words,
  As Masons' tongue affords,
I would, dear Brothers, have rehearsed by *you!,*

King Solomon's Farewell.

It is not difficult to conceive what the parting words of Solomon to his Temple-builders must have been, nor is it strange if tradition has preserved it, in the main, faithfully.

The original PLÁN upon which the architects drafted, was given, we are informed, "in writing by the Spirit," to King David, and by him transferred to his son. This gave the stamp of DIVINITY to the structure. All the after-plans, secondary to the original, were necessarily in accordance with it; so that the Royal Builder might well advise his workmen in the spirit of the following lines:

King Solomon sat in his ivory chair,
His chair on a platform high,
And his words addressed,
Through the listening West,
To a Band of Brothers nigh;
Through the West and South,
These words of truth,
To a Band of Brothers nigh.

" Ye Builders go! ye have done your work—
The CAPSTONE standeth sure;
From the lowermost block,
To the loftiest rock,
The FABRIC is secure;
From the Arch's Swell,
To the Pinnacle,
The FABRIC is secure.

21

"Go, crowned with fame! old time will pass,
　　And many a change will bring,
　　　But the DEED you've done,
　　　The circling sun
　　Through every land will sing;
　　　The moon and stars,
　　　While earth endures,
　　Through every land will sing.

"Go build like this! from the quarries vast,
　　The precious stones reveal;
　　　There's many a block
　　　In the matrice rock,
　　Will honor your fabrics well;
　　　There's many a beam,
　　　By the mountain-stream,
　　Will honor your fabrics well.

"Go build like this! strike off with skill,
　　Each superfluity;
　　　With critic eye,
　　　Each fault espy,
　　Be ZEALOUS, FERVENT, FREE;
　　　By the perfect SQUARE,
　　　Your work prepare—
　　Be ZEALOUS, FERVENT, FREE.

" Go build like this ! to a fitting place,
    Rear up the ASHLARS true ;
       On the Trestleboard
       Of your Master's LORD,
    The GRAND INTENTION view ;
       In each mystic line,
       Of the vast DESIGN,
    The GRAND INTENTION view.

" Go build like this ! and when exact,
    The joinings scarce appear,
       With the Trowel's aid,
       Such cement spread,
    As time can never wear ;
       Lay thickly round,
       Such wise compound,
    As time can never wear.

" Go, Brothers ! thus enjoined, farewell !
    Spread o'er the darkened West ;
       Illume each clime,
       With ART sublime,
    The noblest truths attest ;
       Be MASTERS now,
       And as you go,
    The noblest truths attest !"

Quarry, Hill, and Temple.

The well-known expression in the caption suggests, in the symbolical language of Freemasonry, those various departments of mystical labor in which the speculative craftsmen are employed. To declare one's attachment to his friend, "in quarry, hill, and temple," is to confess a friendship independent of time, place, and circumstances. The ties of Masonry, accepted in the presence of DEITY and under the Divine sanction, are of this nature, and, in a good man's heart, indissoluble.

Thine in the Quarry, whence the stone
For mystic workmanship is drawn:
　　On Jordan's shore,
　　By Zarthan's plain,
Though faint and weary, *thine alone.*
The gloomy mine knows not a ray—
The heavy toil exhausts the day—
　　But love keeps bright
　　The weary heart,
And sings, *I'm thine without decay.*

Thine on the Hill whose cedars rear
Their perfect forms and foliage fair:
　　Each graceful shaft
　　And deathless leaf,
Of Masons' love the emblems are.
Thine when a smile pervades the heaven—
Thine when the sky's with thunder riven—
　　Each echo swells
　　Through answering hills,
My Mason prayer, *for thee 'tis given.*

Thine in the Temple, holy place—
Where silence reigns, the type of peace;
  With grip and sign,
  And mystic line,
My Mason's love I do confess.
Each block we raise, that friendship grows,
Cemented firmly ne'er to loose;
  And when complete,
  The work we greet,
Thine in the joy my bosom knows.

Thine at the midnight in the cave—
Thine in the floats upon the wave—
  By Joppa's hill,
  By Kedron's rill,
And *thine* when Sabbath rest we have.
Yes, yes, dear friend, my spirit saith,
I'm thine until and after death!
  No bounds control
  The Mason's soul
Cemented with a Mason's faith!

Fragrance of a Good Deed.

Many years since, a poor sojourner through the wilds of Texas paused at a farmhouse on the lonely banks of the Brazos, to die. The owner, a Freemason, discovered the Masonic claims of his guest not too late to make the mystic tie available. All the consolations of brotherly sympathy and attendance were freely bestowed upon him, and when these could avail the pilgrim no longer, his remains were tenderly consigned to maternal earth, the generous planter reading the Masonic service and covering in the precious dust, *alone!*

Long years afterwards, and when a populous village had sprung up upon the river banks, a Masonic lodge was established there. The hall was built, and the Mount Moriah upon which it was erected was the green knoll beneath which the stranger's bones are mouldering! Moreton Lodge, No. 72, at Richmond, Texas, yet (1855) stands to perpetuate " the fragrance of a good deed !"

On hallowed ground those walls are reared ;
 That roof encloses in
A spot to Masonry endeared,
 To Zion's Mount, akin ;
Since Zion's Temple is bereft
 And Judah mourns his God,
No holier site on earth is left,
 Than this our feet have trod.

For here, inspired by truest faith,
 Relief a Brother gave—
Upheld a wanderer unto death
 And blessed him with a grave :

Aye, with a grave whose portals closed
  To that majestic song,
Which has to the fraternal host,
  Brought deathless hopes so long.

The EYE DIVINE approved the deed—
  'Tis graven as with steel;
And when the noble act we read
  This fond desire we feel,—
That all *our* mystic work and word
  Thus modeled well may be,
And so the Temple of our God
  Rise fast and gloriously !

A Parting Hymn.

Refreshed with angels' food we go,
To serve Thee in thy work below;
Trusting, when Sabbath-rest is given,
To share Thy richer joys in Heaven.

Then, bind our willing souls in one;
Confirm the COVENANTS here begun;
Each day those vows more sacred be,
Cemented in eternity.

Song for St. John's Day.

These lines have been set to music by Professor Henry Tucker, of New York.

Ended now the Masons' labors,
Past the travel and the toil;
Gather in ye loving neighbors,
Share the Corn, the Wine, the Oil:
　　Brethren now, of each degree,
　　Come in harmony and glee;
　　　　Happy meeting,
　　　　Gentle greeting,—
　　'Tis the joy of Masonry.

Spirits of the blest departed,
As on earthly ways they roam,
Where are met the faithful-hearted,
They to share our labors come;
　　Though their forms we cannot see
　　They are here with you and me.

Love unites us with its cement;
Truth inspires the Masons' breast;
Ever faithful, ever clement,—
Thus our doctrines we attest.
　　Thus we come of each degree,
　　Come in harmony and glee;
　　　　Happy meeting,
　　　　Gentle greeting,—
　　'Tis the joy of Masonry.

23

The Obedient Disciple.

The ancient historian, Jamblichus, describes with unction, the circumstance that forms the basis of the following piece.

The two travelers, therein named, were disciples of Pythagoras, whose system of secret affiliation, if it was not FREEMASONRY, at least exhibited the benevolent features which make up so large a part of it.

A Brother, bound for distant lands,
  In sickness fell alone, alone;
And stranger care from stranger hands,
  Did the last rites of nature own.
But ere the trembling spirit passed,
He on a Tablet faintly traced—

Some mystic lines—a spiral Thread—
  A Square—an emblem of the Sun—
A Chequered Band, that none could read—
  And then his work and life were done.
And stranger care from stranger hands,
Gave him kind burial in the sands.

Full many a year swept by, swept by,
  And the poor stranger was forgot;
While on an olive column, nigh,
  That Tablet marked his burial spot;
And many gazed at Square and Thread,
And many guessed, but none could read.

29

But then a sage Disciple came,
Of one whose wisdom filled the land—
Himself right worthy of the name—
The thoughtful head and ready hand:
He looked upon the mystic lines,
And read the Tablet's full designs.

It spoke of one long passed before,
In quest of truth, like him sincere;
Of one gone onward, never more
To delve in mines deep hidden here;
And solemn was the lesson traced—
Lo Pilgrim! 'tis your fate at last!

Awe-struck, yet wiser now, he strayed
In solemn silence from the spot;
Repaid the debt his brother made,
And Eastward journeyed on his lot;
Yet never on life's shifting wave,
Lost he the lesson of that grave.

How weighty is the charge we give,
Brethren, in this short history read—
To bless the living while we live,
And leave some tokens when we're dead!
On life's broad Tablet let us trace
Emblems to mark *our* burial-place!

Via Lucis, Via Crucis.

"The way of light is the way of the Cross," is one of those ancient maxims which both in rhythm and reason commends itself to the
favor of every reader. The entire System of Freemasonry is an illus-
tration of it.

How *sad to the Grave* are our feet slowly tending,
    The cold form of one whom we loved, on the bier!
What sighs swell our hearts while above him we're bending,
    And shudder to think we must part with him here!
Ah, gloomy is life when our friend has departed!
    Ah, weary the pathway to travel alone!
There's little remaineth to cheer the lone-hearted
    Oppressed with the burden, "the loved one is gone!"

But *glad from the Grave* are our feet homeward tending,
    Though death's cold embraces our Brother restrain!
Hope springs from the hillock above which we're bending,
    And whispers "Rejoice! you shall meet him again!
Death's midnight is sad, but there cometh the morning;
    The pathway is dark but its ending is nigh."
Then patient we wait till the glorious dawning,
    That's told in our emblems of *life in the sky!*

The Beacon-Light.

A city set upon a hill,
    Cannot be hid;
Exposed to every eye, it will,
Over surrounding plain and vale,
    An influence shed,
And spread the light of peace afar,
Or blight the land with horrid war.

Each Masons' lodge is planted so,
    For high display;
Each is a BEACON-LIGHT, to show
Life's weary wanderers, as they go,
    The better way;
To show by ties of earthly love,
How perfect is the Lodge above!

Be this your willing task, dear friends,
    While laboring here;
Borrow from Him who kindly lends,
The HEAVENLY LADDER that ascends
    The higher sphere;
And let the world your progress see,
Upward, by FAITH, HOPE, CHARITY.

Voice of the Temple.

The Voice of the Temple! the tidings of Love,
That speaks of the MASTER who reigneth above;
"HIS GLORY, HIS GLORY, in the Highest who dwells,
And GOOD-WILL TO MAN" is the burden it tells!
      Come Brothers, in chorus
      Prolong the glad tidings,
No duty so sweet as the hymning of God:
      His faith each professing,
      His knowledge possessing,
Exalt each the blessing His grace hath bestowed.

Building the Fane.

The cry of Nehemiah, when, on his return to Jerusalem, he saw the ROYAL CITY lying "heaps upon heaps," has, in every age, echoed upon the heart of the moral builder. Oh, the world in ruins! oh, the wrecks of humanity, lying about us on every hand, and crying aloud for the MASTER BUILDER, who alone can reconstruct the edifice so fearfully cast down!

      Come, Comrades, let us build! *
      Our Mason-hearts are filled
With fond solicitude and keen desire, †
      While musing o'er these heaps,
      Whose every ashlar keeps
The stains of bloodshed and the marks of fire! ‡

What though some voice would say
"Leave Salem to decay!" §
Our Mason-hearts were not instructed thus:
Let's work for Salem's Lord,—
And, Comrades, be assured
The God of Heaven, HE will prosper us! |

With goodly SWORD and bright,
With TROWEL in the right,
Each hand is sanctified to God's employ: ¶
Let's build, nor doubt that soon—
This weary labor done—
Our Mason-hearts will feel the BUILDER's joy! **

---

* Come and let us build up the wall of Jerusalem, that we be no more a reproach.
—*Nehemiah*, ii., 17.

† I sat down and wept, and mourned, and fasted, and prayed.—*Nehemiah*, i., 4.

‡ They slew with the sword young man and maiden, old man, and him that stooped for age, and they burnt the house of God and all the palaces with fire.—2 *Chronicles* xxxvi., 17, 19.

§ Sanballat and Tobiah and Geshem laughed us to scorn, and despised us and said, What is this thing that ye do?—*Nehemiah*, ii., 19.

| I answered and said unto them, "The God of Heaven, He will prosper us, therefore, we His servants will arise and build."—*Nehemiah*, ii., 20.

¶ Every one with *one* of his hands wrought in the work, and with the *other* hand held a weapon.—*Nehemiah*, iv., 17.

** They sang together by course in praising and giving thanks, and all the people shouted with a great shout, because the foundation of the house of the Lord was laid.—*Ezra*. iii., 11.

Hymn of the Mason-Soldiers.

In camp, hospital, and on the march, the "Friends of the Square" in the Union armies, were wont, during the campaigns of the fall and winter of 1863, to enliven the sad hours by singing this "Hymn of the Mason-Soldiers," as arranged to Professor Henry Tucker's unequaled melody, "When this Cruel War is Over."

Brothers, met from every nation,
    Far away from home,
Men of every rank and station,
    Round this altar come.
Bring your hearts, so full of feeling;
    Join your hands, so true;
Swear, ye sons of truth and honor,
    Naught shall sever you.

Chorus.—War's dark cloud will vanish—
    Joy to EAST and WEST,
      Oh, Brothers!
    Though the land is full of weeping,
    Masons, Masons still are blest.

Come, forgetting every sorrow,
    LEVEL bring and SQUARE;
Leave all trouble to to-morrow;
    Each the COMPASS bear;
Pass the TROWEL o'er each discord;
    Wear the LAMBSKIN white;
Brothers, one more happy meeting,
    In our Lodge to-night.

In the circle here extended,
  Shadowy forms appear;
With our loving spirits blended,
  Dead ones, ah, how dear!
Dead on many a field of battle,
  Lost to friends and home,
Yet in Mason's love surviving,
  Round this altar come.

When to distant homes returning,
  We shall say farewell,
And shall cease the tender yearning,
  Now our bosoms feel—
Prattling lips and sweet caresses,
  All the joys of home,
Will bring back the loving circle,
  Round this altar come.

Earnestness of Covenanting.

Never will I break the Covenant,
  Plighted, Brother, with thee now!
ONE between us stands, attesting
  To the fervor of my vow:
In his name, *above* his Promise,
  By his honor, *for* his cause,
Here's my hand, the Lord confirm it,—
  I will surely keep my vows!

The Fervor of Affiliation.

The privilege of association in a harmonious, strongly-cemented band of Masons, is a thing to be coveted. Exiles from home, deprived of the long-accustomed pleasures of the lodge, have been known to express their yearnings for re-affiliation in language not less forcible than this. In the military camps, these lines sung to the common air "A Life on the Ocean Wave," are very popular.

A place in the Lodge for me,
A home with the free and bright,
Where jarring chords agree,
And the darkest soul is light:
Not here, not here is bliss,
There's turmoil and there's gloom;
My spirit yearns for peace—
Say, Brothers, say, is there room!

My feet are weary worn,
And my eyes are dim with tears;
This world is all forlorn,
A wilderness of fears;
But *there's one green spot below*,
There's a resting place, a home,
My spirit yearns to know—
Say, Brothers, say, is there room!

I hear the orphan's cry,
And I see the widow's tear;
I weep when mortals die,
And none but God is near;

87

From sorrow and despair,
I seek the Mason's home,
My spirit yearns to share—
Say, Brothers, say, is there room!

With God's own eye above,
With BROTHER-HANDS below,
With FRIENDSHIP and with LOVE.
My pilgrimage I'll go;
And when in death's embrace,
My summons it shall come,
Within your heart's best place,
Oh, Brothers, oh give me room!

The Enclosure.

FROM ME TO THEE, FROM ME TO THEE,
    Each whispering leaf a missive be,
In mystic scent and hue to say—
    This green and fragrant spray—
In emerald green and rich perfume,
    To teach of FAITH that mocks the tomb,
And link the chain FIDELITY,
    'Twixt, Brother, thee and me!

In distant land, in olden time,
    The ACACIA bore the mark sublime,
And told to each discerning eye
    Of deathless constancy:

So may these green leaves whisper now,
  Inform the heart, inspire the vow,
And link the chain FIDELITY,
  'Twixt, Brother, thee and me!

Masonic Training.

Oh! Ladies, when you bend above,
The cradled offspring of your love,
And bless the child whom you would see
A man of truth and constancy,—
Believe, there is in Masons' lore,
A fund of wisdom, beauty, power,
Enriching every soul of man
Who comprehends the mystic plan.

Then train your boy in Mason's truth;
Lay deep the cornerstone in youth;
Teach him to walk by virtue's line,
To square his acts by SQUARE DIVINE;
The cement of pure love to spread,
And paths of Scripture-truth to tread;
Then will the Youth to manhood grow
To honor *us* and honor *you.*

Ask! Seek!! Knock!!!

Ask, and ye shall receive;
  Seek, ye shall surely find;
Knock, ye shall no resistance meet,
  If come with ready mind;
For all that ask, and ask aright,
Are welcome to our lodge to-night.

Lay down the bow and spear;
  Resign the sword and shield;
Forget the arts of warfare here,
  The arms of peace to wield;
For all that seek, and seek aright,
Are welcome to our lodge to-night.

Bring hither thoughts of peace;
  Bring hither words of love;
Diffuse the pure and holy joy
  That cometh from above;
For all that knock, and knock aright,
Are welcome to our lodge to-night.

Ask help of Him that's high;
  Seek grace of Him that's true;
Knock patiently, the hand is nigh,
  Will open unto you;
For all that ask, seek, knock aright,
Are welcome to our lodge to-night.

Masonic Auld-Lang-Syne.

A society whose ceremonies and language extend so far into antiquity as those of Freemasonry, may justly claim, more than others, to be *the conservator of old things*. Nowhere are aged men so prized as in lodges of Freemasons. The models of lodge furniture, to the smallest piece, are of ancient patterns, and their lectures and their songs, and their hopes, all breathe the spirit so well expressed in the Scotch phrase, "Auld Lang Syne." The following lines, much used in the gatherings of the Craft, may be accompanied in recitation with significant gestures.

We do not sigh for pleasures past,
  Nor fondly, vainly pine;
Yet let us give one memory
  To Auld Lang Syne.

With Gavel, Trowel, Guage, we work,
  With Level, Square, and Line;
Come, join the CHAIN OF LOVE, and sing
  Of Auld Lang Syne!
For Auld Lang Syne, my dear,
  For Auld Lang Syne;
Ah, who like us can sing the days
  Of Auld Lang Syne!

'Twas sweet when evening's shadows fell—
  How bright our Lights did shine!
Down from the East to hear the words
  Of Auld Lang Syne.

The 'PRENTICE knocked with trembling hand,
  The CRAFT sought Corn and Wine,
The MASTER stood, and nobly fell,
  In Auld Lang Syne.

With step so true, with form upright,
  We drew the GRAND DESIGN;
'Twas well we knew "to square the work,"
  In Auld Lang Syne.

A tear to them, THE EARLY DEAD,
  Fond memory would consign;
We dropped the green sprig o'er their head,
  In Auld Lang Syne.

And till the MASTER call us hence
  To join the LODGE DIVINE,
Let's sometimes give a grateful thought
  To Auld Lang Syne!

Tears and Smiles.

The *tear* for friends departed,
  The faithful and true-hearted,
Cast midst the rubbish of the silent grave,
  Is changed to *smiles* of pleasure,
  While trusting that our treasure,
A glorious Resurrection-day will have!

Nunc Dimittis.

It is written of a venerable Craftsman of the past generation, that, having lived through all the trials and reproaches of the Antimasonic period (1826–1836), and maintained his membership first in one lodge and then in another, as the contiguous lodges successively gave way under the pressure, he came peacefully to his death-bed at last, and, smilingly said to the friends who thronged about his bed-side, " Now, Brothers, let me have my demit !"

In the oldest system of Masonic ethics extant, it is distinctly averred that " every Brother ought to belong to a lodge." The practice of non-affiliation so common at the present day, is thus stamped as unmasonic. Death alone should sever lodge-affiliation.

" Now dismiss me, while I linger,
   For one fond, one dear word more ;
Have I done my labor fairly ?
   Is there aught against my score ?
Have I wronged in all this circle,
   One by deed, or word, or blow ?—
Silence speaks my full acquittance—
   Nunc dimittis, let me go !

" Let me go, I crave my wages ;
   Long I've suffered, long I've toiled ;
Never once through work days idle,
   Never once my apron soiled ;
In the CHAMBER, where the Master
   Waits with smiling to bestow
CORN, and WINE, and OIL abundant,
   Nunc dimittis, let me go !

43

"Let me go, but *you* must tarry,
  Till the Sixth day's close has come;
Heat and burden patient bear ye
  While you're absent far from home;
But a little for the summons
  Waits alike for each of you;—
Mine is sounding, spirits wait me,
  Nunc dimittis, let me go!

"Oh, the Sabbath-day in Heaven!
  Oh, the joys reserved for them,
Faithful Builders of the Temple,
  Type of blest Jerusalem!
Oh, the raptures of the meeting
  With the friends 'twas bliss to know!
Strive no longer to detain me,
  Nunc dimittis, let me go!"

Hushed that voice its fond imploring;
  Faded is that eager eye;
Gone the soul of labor wearied,
  To repose eternally:
But the memory of his service
  Oft shall lighten up our woe,
Till the hour *we too* petition—
  "*Nunc dimittis*, let me go!"

Lingering Notes.

None of the ancient Masonic legends are more graceful or convey a more charmingly esoteric meaning, than that which assures us there is for an hour after the Brethren disperse from their lodge-room *a mysterious echo of sounds* which may be heard there, weird, lingering, fraternal in tone, made up, in fact, of all the brotherly expressions and divine acknowledgments that have passed about the group through the entire convocation! It is affirmed by those who have the gift to understand it, to be charming beyond expression, and that the last note, as it dies away upon the ear, is the echo of that spirit which filled the soul of our Patron Saint, the Evangelist John—"Love!"

Lingering notes the echoes stir,
　　Soft and sweet, these walls along;
Softly, sweetly, they concur
　　In the pleasant tide of song;
Night-birds cease their plaintive lays
Listening to the hymn of praise.

Angels gliding through the air,
　　On celestial mission bent,
Pause, the sacred hymn to hear—
　　Fold their wings in soft content—
Join their notes divine to these,
Hymning Masons' mysteries.

Now the solitary room,
　　Peopled with a countless throng—
Now the stillness and the gloom
　　Kindle with the tide of song,
Filling our delighted ears—
Music of three thousand years!

45

Every Emblem pictured there,
  On the ceiling, wall, or floor—
GAVEL, TROWEL, APRON, SQUARE,
  COLUMN rent or open DOOR—
Blends a light and yields a tongue,
To this softly-lingering song.

Now the anthem dies away;
  One by one the voices cease;
Birds resume their wonted lay;
  Angels on their mission press;
But the latest note that moves
In the mystic song is LOVE'S!

————

The Giving of the Shoe.

Take this pledge! it is a token
Of that truth that ne'er was broken,
Truth which binds the Mystic Tie,
Under the All-Seeing Eye.

Take this pledge! each ancient Brother,
By this type bound every other
Firmly, so that death, alone,
Rent the bonds that made them one.

Take this pledge! no pledge so holy;
Though the symbol seem but lowly,
'Tis divine! It tells of ONE,
Of the rain-drops and the sun.

Take this pledge! the token sealeth
All the judgment-day revealeth;
Honor, Truth, fraternal Grace,
Brother, in thy hands I place!

Inscriptions for a Lodge-Room.

EAST.

Erect before thee,
    A hand upon thy WORD,
We thus adore thee
    And swear to serve thee, Lord!

WEST.

So mote it be—each murmuring word
Speaks the soul's earnest, deep accord,
And echoes, from its inmost sea,
A deep "AMEN, SO MOTE IT BE!"

SOUTH.

Ye faithful, weave the chain!
    Join hand in hand again!
The world is filled with violence and blood!
    Hark to the battle-cry!
    Hark to the answering sigh!
Come weave the chain that's blest of man and God!

The Pillars of the Porch.

An innovation upon the Masonic landmarks is like removing one of the emblems from the Pillars at the entrance of the Temple. It is Masonic sacrilege. Every instructed brother will set himself resolutely against such an act, remembering the declaration in the ancient books of our Order: "It is not in the power of any man or body of men to make innovations in the body of Masonry." In this lie the STRENGTH and the ESTABLISHMENT of the Order.

The OLD is better : is it not the plan
    By which the WISE, in by-gone days, contrived
To bind in willing fetters man to man,
    And strangers in a sacred nearness lived ?
Is there in modern wisdom aught like that
    Which, midst the blood and carnage of the plain,
Can calm man's fury, mitigate his hate,
    And join disrupted friends in love again ?

No ! for three thousand years the smiles of heaven,
    Smiles on whose sunbeams comes unmeasured joy,
To this thrice-honored CEMENT have been given,
    This BOND, this COVENANT, this sacred TIE :
It comes to us full laden : from the Tomb
    A countless host conspire to name its worth,
Who sweetly sleep beneath th' ACACIA's bloom,—
    And there is nought like Masonry on earth.

Then guard the venerable relic well ;
    Protect it, Masters, from th' unholy hand ;
See that its emblems the same lessons tell
    Sublime through every age and every land ;

48

Be not a line erased; the pen that drew
These matchless tracings was the PEN DIVINE;—
Infinite Wisdom best for mortals knew—
God will preserve intact the GRAND DESIGN.

———

Cherishing the Pledge.

During the Civil War, the question, How far the Masonic obligations extend to those in arms against their country, has perplexed many. The following Ode is proposed as the ancient and sure solution of the difficulty. The ANCIENT CHARGES, it will be found, leave no room for doubt upon the subject.

It would be criminal here to omit to state the fact that through all the strife which has deluged the land in blood, while other bonds and covenants have been nullified, the BOND OF FREEMASONRY has remained intact !

Dear Friends of the Square *let us cherish our faith,*
Though broken and torn every other !
REMEMBER THE VOW ;—we swore unto death
We would cling, *hand and heart,* to a Brother !
   Then raise up to God the left hand !
      With mine join the other !
   Though war blow the blast, and with death strew the land,
      WE SWEAR TO BE TRUE TO EACH BROTHER !

The EAST lends his light, though the world is at war;
The SOUTH shines in glory and beauty ;
The WEST gently smiles o'er fields drenched in gore—
They teach to each Mason his duty !

The Badge of the Craft is unsullied as yet—
From war's dust and blood let us fold it!
The Page of our History is brilliant with light;⌣
Let's swear thus in honor to hold it!

GREAT GOD! from thy Throne view the nation at strife!
THY GAVEL must heal this disorder!
Send Peace o'er the land! give Refuge and Life!
Be THOU LORD our Saviour and Warder!
    Then raise up to God the left hand!
      With mine join the other!
    Though war blow the blast, and with death strew the land,
      WE SWEAR TO BE TRUE TO EACH BROTHER!

Let Your Light Shine.

"Let your light shine," the Master said,—
    "To bless benighted man!
The light and truth my Spirit shed
    Are yours to shed again."

We come, oh Lord, with willing mind,
    That knowledge to display;
Enlighten us, by nature blind,
    And glad we will obey.

Brotherly Love.

By one GOD created, by one SAVIOUR saved,
By one SPIRIT lighted, by one MARK engraved,
We're taught in the wisdom our spirits approve,
To cherish the spirit of BROTHERLY LOVE.
      Love, love, Brotherly love—
This world has no spirit like Brotherly love.

In the land of the stranger we Masons abide,
In forest, in quarry, on Lebanon's side;
Yon temple we're building, its plan's from above,
And we labor supported by BROTHERLY LOVE.

Though the service be hard, and the wages be scant,
If the MASTER accept it, our hearts are content:
The prize that we toil for, we'll have it above,
When the Temple's completed, in BROTHERLY LOVE.

Yes, yes, though the week may be long, it will end,—
Though the temple be lofty, THE KEYSTONE will stand:
And the SABBATH, blest day, every thought will remove,
Save the mem'ry fraternal of BROTHERLY LOVE.

By one GOD created,—come, brothers, 'tis day!
By one SPIRIT lighted—come, brothers, away!
With Beauty, and Wisdom, and Strength to approve,
Let's toil while there's labor in BROTHERLY LOVE.

51

The Fire of Friendship.

Nothing in the Masonic institution is more practical or more grateful to the sensibilities of the traveling-brother than to find, as he will do in every lodge in this country an officer whose constitutional duty it is "to welcome and accommodate visiting brethren." This makes the circle of the Order complete, for every well-informed brother has a claim and a right to the hospitalities of lodges wherever he may travel or work. The following lines represent the sentiments of gratitude which such an one may be supposed to feel upon the reception of that broad and unreserved welcome peculiar to the Masonic system.

Men of the bright inheritance, oh true and loving band,
Who, linked in chains of Masonry, around this altar stand,
Bright let THE FIRE OF FRIENDSHIP burn and warmly let it glow,
For a stranger from a distant land would join your circle now.

THE ACACIA blooms in every clime, the BROKEN SHAFT doth
        rear
Its mournful form in mystic guise, and meets us everywhere;
The GAVEL rings o'er land and sea, yon EMBLEM speaks the same,
About the globe, as here it speaks, THE UNIVERSAL NAME.

And why? because ONE GOD we have in whom alone we trust;
He made us all, OUR FATHER made us all of kindred dust;
The same green MOTHER EARTH, the broad, the generous he
        gave,
That feeds us while we live and gives us when we die, a grave.

We build a common TEMPLE too, the lofty and the low,
We bring the same heart-offerings and in common homage bow;
Our TRACING-BOARD the same designs in every clime has given,
And, serving the same MASTER, we expect the same bright
    HEAVEN.

Then let the stranger have a place within your mystic band,
Where eye responsive answers eye, and hand unites with hand;
He knows your WORD, he knows your SIGN, he asks no better
    grace
Than with you here to sit awhile and greet you face to face.

Peace in the lodges where you work be heaven's boon to-day;
Peace, Peace;—it is the yearning prayer the stranger's heart
    would pray;
And could they hear it from the land and from the rolling sea,
From every Mason's lips would come the cry, So MOTE IT BE!

Words of Peace and Love.

Now, while the Thunder-peal of battle is heard,
Earth with the trampling of legions is stirred,
Turn from the Battle, Brothers, take from above,
    WORDS OF PEACE AND LOVE!
  Hearts of consolation, bide ye the vow!
  Hands, never weary in charity now!
  Tongues rich in sympathy, oh take from above
    WORDS OF PEACE AND LOVE.

Blood like a river flowing, smokes o'er the plain;
Tears, bitter weeping—oh, who can refrain!
Stay, stay the slaughter, Brothers, stay this distress,
Speak the WORDS OF PEACE!

Thus speaks the TROWEL, Brothers, thus speaks the LINE,
Thus speaks the COMPASS and SYMBOL DIVINE;
Each bears its message on the white wings of Peace,
Bids all warrings cease.

———

The Pilgrim's Home.

In the "Life in the Triangle," is described a MASONIC BURIAL AT
NIGHT, of which this Ode forms a part. Four members of the fraternity, who resided in an intensely antimasonic community, had discovered the body of a man upon whose garments was seen the mystic emblem of the Order. This they had carefully enshrouded and provided
with a coffin. At night, with every precaution against interruption,
they took it to the village graveyard and interred it, with the songs
and the signs, and the circuits prescribed by the time-honored usage.

Bear him home, his bed is made
In the stillness, in the shade;
Day has parted, night has come,
Bear the Brother to his home—
Bear him home.

Bear him home, no more to roam,
Bear the tired Pilgrim home;
Forward! all his toils are o'er—
Home where journeying is no more—
　　Bear him home.

Lay him down; his bed is here;
See the dead are resting near!
Brothers they their Brothers own,
Lay the wanderer gently down—
　　Lay him down.

Lay him down; let nature spread
Starry curtains o'er the dead;
Lay him down; let angel eyes
View him kindly from the skies—
　　Lay him down.

Ah, not yet for us the bed,
Where the faithful Pilgrim's lain!
Pilgrims weep, again to go
Through life's weariness and woe—
　　Ah, not yet!

Soon 'twill come, if faithful here,
Soon the end of all our care;
Strangers here, we seek a HOME,
FRIENDS and SAVIOUR in the tomb—
　　Soon 'twill come.

Let us go, and on our way
Faithful journey, faithful pray;
Through the sunshine, through the snow,
Boldly, Brother Pilgrims, go—
  Let us go.

Hymn for Consecration.

Lo, God is here, our prayers prevail!
In deeper reverence adore;
ASK FREELY NOW! he will not fail
His largest, richest gifts to pour.

Ask by these EMBLEMS old and true;
Ask by the memories of the past;
Ask by HIS OWN GREAT NAME, for lo,
His every promise there is cast!.

Ask WISDOM! 'tis the chiefest thing:
Ask STRENGTH, such strength as GOD may yield;
Ask BEAUTY from his Throne to spring
And grace the Temple we shall build.

LORD GOD MOST HIGH, our LODGE we veil!
'Tis CONSECRATE with ancient care;
Oh let THY SPIRIT ever dwell,
And guide the loving BUILDERS here!

The White-aproned Brothers.

And he said unto me, What are these which are arrayed in white robes, and whence came they? And I said unto him, Sir, thou knowest. And he said unto me, These are they which came out of great tribulation, and have washed their robes, and have made them white in the blood of the Lamb.

Therefore are they before the throne of God, and serve him day and night in his temple; and he that sitteth on the throne shall dwell among them.

They shall hunger no more, neither thirst any more; neither shall the sun light on them nor any heat.

For the Lamb which is in the midst of the throne shall feed them, and shall lead them unto living fountains of waters; and God shall wipe away all tears from their eyes.—*Rev.* vii., 13–17.

Come cease from your labors,
Ye white-aproned neighbors,
And answer my words—
Tell us *who are ye?*
" We are friends of humanity,
Hating profanity,
Spurning all vanity,
CHILDREN OF PEACE—
Men who can feel
All our *own* need of kindness,
And bless the GREAT GOD,
Who hath lightened our blindness."

Tell us, *what do ye?*
" By precept, example,
  We're building a temple,
  Fair, lofty and ample
      For HIM whom we serve—
      Following the plans
  That our MASTER doth give us,
      And amply repaid
  When His servants receive us."

And *what do you work with?*
" The Gage and the Gavel,
  The Plumb, Square and Level,
  And then as we travel,
      The Trowel we hold—
      Skillfully these,
  As first we're inducted—
      Obediently these,
  In the way we're instructed."

Your timbers, what are they?
" The blocks that we quarry,
  And timbers so heavy,
  Our hands shape and carry,
      Those ashlars are MEN;
      Rough ashlars they are—
  But hewed, marked and garnished,
      By precepts divine,
  Our task will be finished."

Your resting, when is it?
" We look for no leisure,
  We sigh for no pleasure,
  We covet no treasure,
    Till SATURDAY NIGHT—
   Wages and joys,
And a rest without breaking,
  Wait for us then,
In the home that we're seeking."

Hours of Praise.

Morn, the morn, sweet morn is springing;
  In the East his sign appears;
Dews, and songs, and fragrance flinging
  Down the new robe nature wears.
Forth from slumber, forth and meet him!
  Who too dead to love and light?
Forth, and as you stand to greet him,
  Praise to HIM who giveth night.

Noon, the noon, high noon is glowing;
  In the South rich glories burn;
Beams intense from Heaven are flowing;
  Mortal eye must droop and turn.

Forth and meet him! while the chorus
  Of the groves is nowhere heard,
Kneel to HIM who bendeth o'er us—
  Praise with heart and willing word.

Eve, the eve, still eve is weeping;
  In the West she dies away;
Every winged one is sleeping—
  They've no life but open day.
Forth and meet her! lo, she lends us
  Thrice ten thousand brilliants high!
Glory to HIS name who sends us
  Such night-jewels from the sky.

Death, pale death, to all is certain;
  From the grave his voice comes up—
" Fearless raise my gloomy curtain—
  Find within, eternal hope":
Forth and meet HIM, ye whose duty
  To the LORD OF LIFE is given:
HE will clothe death's garb with beauty—
  HE will give a path to Heaven.

The Dying Hope.

ALGERNON SYDNEY was executed on the scaffold, Dec. 7, 1683. Having ended his devotions, he placed his head, unassisted, on the block. Being asked by the headsman, according to custom, " Sir, will you rise again ?" he answered promptly and unfalteringly, " Not till the GENERAL RESURRECTION ! Strike on !"

On the verge of Eternity, calmly surveying
    The dark-rolling waters that threatened beneath,
The MARTYR OF LIBERTY ended his praying,
    And patiently waited the signal of death;
His head on the block, but his spirit away,
In the land where the tyrant shall forfeit his sway.

The words of his lips, how undaunted and cheering !
    They spoke of a victory grand and complete ;
They told that this mortal, whom despots were fearing,
    Though conquered by wrong, was the conquerer yet—
"The grave cannot hold me ! the dust shall be won
From the worm and the darkness of nature ! STRIKE ON !"

How mighty that hope, when the spirit departing,
    Must sunder the ties that have bound it so long,
To feel that this tenement we are deserting,
    Shall rise to new glories thro' JESUS THE STRONG !
The grave cannot hold us ! the flesh shall be won
From the worm and the darkness of nature ! STRIKE ON !

Ah, yes! and each flaw that the eye has detected,
    While occupied here shall be covered above;
Renewed by the same glorious hand that erected,
    These Temples shall all be made perfect in love;
The grave shall not hold us—this flesh shall be won
From the worm and the darkness of nature! STRIKE ON!

Then cheer Brothers, cheer! for why *should* death alarm us!
    A brief separation the monster will bring;
His pangs will afford, though a moment they harm us,
    A glorious reunion thro' Jesus the King!
The grave shall not hold us—this flesh shall be won
From the worm and the darkness of nature! STRIKE ON!

Ono.

In the eleventh chapter of Nehemiah, the expression " Ono, the
valley of Craftsmen" occurs, which forms the subject of the following
lines:

    Where is the true heart's MOTHER-LODGE?
    Is't where, perchance he earliest heard
    The frightful voice, from rocky ledge,
    That told a horrid deed of blood?
    Is't where his vision earliest saw,
    And hands enclasped that GOLDEN THING,
    The symbol-crowned, the wondrous LAW,
    Noblest creation of our King?

No: though in fancy he may turn,
In pleasing reminiscence back,
As happiest hearts at times, will yearn,
To tread again youth's flowery track,—
The true heart's MOTHER-LODGE is found
Where truest, fondest hearts conspire
To draw love's deathless chain around,
And kindle up love's deathless fire.

Methinks that *here*, dear Friends, must be,
ONO, the Craftsmen's happy VALE,
Ahd *you*, true Laborer, brave and free
The MASTER in the peaceful dale!
So let me fancy and when bowed
In daily adorations due,
I will entreat the Masons' God
To bless the Craftsmen here, and *you!*

Pledge to a Dying Brother.

We'll lay thee down when thou shalt sleep,
    All tenderly and brotherly;
And woman's eyes with ours shall weep
    The precious drops of sympathy:
We'll spread above thee cedar boughs
    Whose emerald hue and rich perfume
Shall make thee deem thy resting-place
    A balmy bed and not a tomb.

That teeming breast which has supplied
    Thy wants from earliest infancy,
Shall open fondly and supply
    Unbroken rest and sleep to thee :
Each spring the flower roots shall send up
    Their painted emblems toward the sky,
To bid thee wait, within thy couch,
    A little longer patiently.

We'll not forget thee, we who stay
    To work a little longer here ;
Thy name, thy faith, thy love shall lie
    On memory's page all bright and clear ;
And when o'erwearied by the toil
    Of life, our heavy limbs shall be,
We'll come and one by one lie down
    Upon dear mother-earth with thee.

And there we'll slumber by thy side ;
    There, reunited 'neath the sod
We'll wait, nor doubt in HIS good time
    To feel the raising-hand of GOD !
To be translated from the earth,
    This land of sorrow and complaints,
To the ALL-PERFECT LODGE ABOVE
    Whose MASTER is the King of Saints.

A Look to the Orient.

Yes, in yon world of perfect light,
   The wearied soul at last may rest;
No higher, farther, wings its flight,
   Brought to the glories *of the East.*

There is the long-sought boon divine,
   And worthy of the painful quest;
When evening shades of life decline,
   The day is dawning *in the East.*

Who feels this truth in fervent heart,
   May know his last hours are his best;
How joyful from *the West* to part
   When calls the Master *from the East.*

Join hearts and hands in union dear—
   Jesus has sanctified the test;
Life's chain is only broken here
   To join forever *in the East.*

Mourners, your tears with gladness blend!
   Joy, Brothers, joy, our faith's confessed!
The grave will yield our parted friend,
   When we with him *approach the East.*

Prayer—Oral or Secret.

There is a prayer unsaid—
No lips its accents move;
'Tis uttered by the pleading eye,
And registered above.

Each MYSTIC SIGN is prayer,
By hand of Mason given;
Each gesture pleads or imprecates
And is observed in heaven.

The deeds that mercy prompts,
Are prayers in sweet disguise;
Though unobserved by any here,
They're witnessed in the skies.

Then at the altar kneel—
In silence make thy prayer;
And HE whose very name is LOVE
The plea will surely hear.

The darkest road is light—
We shun the dangerous snare,
When heavenly hand conducts the road,
Responsive to our prayer.

66

The Song of St. John.

How blest is the home
Where the Brotherhood come!
How charming the time and occasion!
The love that was born,
In the heart of Saint John,
Now warms up the heart of each Mason.

It is you, Sir, and you,
Friendly Brothers and true,
No matter what may be your station—
On the level our way,
WE ARE EQUAL TO-DAY,
For I, Sirs, with you, am a Mason!

This love that was born,
In the heart of St. John,
Is the bond of a charming connexion;
Through good, and through ill,
It abides with us still,
And makes us *thank God we're a Mason.*

When in the Lodge met,
And the officers set,
'Tis of duty and pleasure the season,
Ah! gladly is given
To the FATHER IN HEAVEN,
The praises devout of each Mason.

When labor is done,
And the Brotherhood gone,
Do you think that our secrets we blazon ?
No ! no, 'tis the joy
Of our mystic employ,
That we tell them to none but a Mason.

For 'tis this we do learn,
From our patron St. John,
The pride of this charming occasion,
That the tongue that conceals,
And never reveals,
Is THE VERY BEST THING FOR A MASON !

Then Lady and Sir,
While we stoutly aver,
In our Secrets we'll never work treason,
The rules we profess,
Are the same that did grace
Our patron ST. JOHN, THE FREEMASON.

And while to his *name*,
We may boldly lay claim,
To his *graces* we'll cling till death's season,
And then to the bourne,
Where his spirit has gone,
We'll hie us like every good Mason.

Tribute to Washington.

Ho! Brothers of the MYSTIC TIE,
  Come round me if you please!
Lay down the GAVEL and the SQUARE,
  And let the TROWEL cease;
The work may stop a little while—
  The Master will not blame,
While I from memory sing of one
  Right worthy of the name,—
    A true old-time Freemason
    Whose name was WASHINGTON!

Of every superfluity
  He did his mind divest;
He would not set a timber up
  Unless it was the best:
He plumbed, and squared, and leveled well
  His BLOCKS, and set them true;
Then turned his apron MASTER-WISE
  And spread the mortar due—
    This true old-time Freemason
    Whose name was WASHINGTON!

When bloody war at foreign hands,
  His country threatened sore,
He thought it *right* to take the sword,
  And guard his native shore;

He stood where bravest hearts are found—
　He struck for liberty ;
But when the conquered foemen sued,
　A man of mercy he—
　　This true old-time Freemason,
　　The glorious WASHINGTON.

Upon his Apron was no stain ;
　His work had no defect ;
The OVERSEER accepted all,
　There was nothing to reject.
He lived in peace with God and man ;
　He died in glorious hope,
That CHRIST, the LION, JUDAH'S PRIDE,
　Would raise his body up—
　　This true old-time Freemason,
　　OUR BROTHER WASHINGTON.

———

The Broken Column.

"His WORK was not done, yet his Column is broken ;"
Mourn ye and weep, for ye cherished his worth ;
Let every tear-drop be sympathy's token,—
Lost to the Brotherhood, lost to the earth.

His WORK had been planned by a WISDOM SUPERNAL ;
Strength had been given him meet for the same ;
Down in the midst he is fallen, and vernal
Leaves hang above him and whisper his fame.

His WORK WAS TO BUILD; on the walls we beheld him—
Swiftly and truly they rose 'neath his hand;'
Envious death with his Gavel has felled him,
Plumb-line and Trowel are strewn o'er the land.

His WORK thus unfinished to *us* is entrusted;
MASTER OF MASONS, give strength we entreat,
Bravely to work with these Implements rusted,
Wisely to build till the Temple's complete!

A Mason's Epitaph.

His epitaph a Mason true and good,
Sincere in friendship, ready in relief,
Discreet in trusts, faithful in Brotherhood,
Tender in sympathy and kind in grief.

On grateful memories his name is writ;
His genial heart *our* hearts did kindle up;
We drew our inspiration from his light
And buoyancy from his all-buoyant hope.

His toils are ended; *we* must labor on :
OUR MASTER for a little longer calls
Our hands to *duty* at the rising sun,
Our hearts to *rest* when evening shadow falls.

But 'twill be ended soon ; may our reward
Be upon hearts like his to lie secure ;
Like him to enjoy the favor of the LORD,
Whose grace is boundless and whose promise sure.

Death, the Celestial Gate.

By the pallid hue of those
Whose sweet blushes mocked the rose—
By the fixed, unmeaning eye,
Sparkled once so cheerfully—

By the cold damps on the brow—
By the tongue, discordant now—
By the gasp and laboring breath,
What! oh tell us, what is death!

By the vacancy of heart,
Where the lost one had a part—
By the yearning to retrieve
Treasures hidden in the grave—

By the future, hopeless all,
Wrapped as in a funeral pall—
By the links that rust beneath,
What! oh tell us, what is death!

By the echoes swelled around,
Sigh and moan and sorrow-sound—
By the grave that, opened nigh,
Cruel, yields us no reply—

By the silent king, whose dart
Seeks and finds the mortal part,
We may know, *no human breath*
Can inform us what is death!

But the grave *has* spoken loud !
Once was raised the pallid shroud ;
When the stone was rolled away—
When the earth, in frenzy's play—

Shook her pillars to awake
Him who suffered for our sake;
When the vail's deep fissure showed
All the mysteries of God!

Tell us, then, thou grave of hope,
What is He that breaks thee up?
"Mortal, from my chambers dim,
CHRIST AROSE, inquire of him!"

Hark, unto the earnest cry,
Notes celestial make reply !
"Christian, unto thee 'tis given—
DEATH'S A PASSAGE UNTO HEAVEN!"

Burns' Farewell.

*As sung by Professor John C. Baker, the vocalist, there is a pathos
in Burns' celebrated Ode that is irresistible.*

Never since 'neath the daisies laid
Burns joined the cold and tuneless dead,
Were those sweet lines, his noblest flight,
Sung as you sung them o'er last night.

They bore us, fancy-winged, above;
They thrilled the inmost soul with love;
And tears confessed "The fond Adieu"
As sung so well, last night, by you.

Ah what a thing is this to spread,
That binds the living with the dead,
And makes them *one fraternal throng*
As you, last night, so justly sung!

How blest are we who rightly claim
The Masons' heart, the Masons' name,
And see "the Hieroglyphic bright"
Of which you sung, so well, last night!

Then as you journey sweetly sing;
Let craftsmen hear that tuneful thing;
No better can the pen indite
Than those sweet words you sung last night.

74

And when your own HIGH XII. has come,
And craftsmen bear you, weeping, home,
May loving friends *your* requiem write
Like those grand words you sung last night !

The Crescent.

Addressed to Crescent Lodge, No. 402, City of New York.

GROWING, GROWING still in NUMBERS,
  Still in living stones of strength ;
Some on earth, and some in Heaven,
  Where you may arrive at length :
While the Moon its horns shall fill,
" CRESCENT " be your motto still !

GROWING, GROWING still in WISDOM,
  Light still breaking day by day,
Sacred light from yonder volume
  Leading to the perfect way !
While the Moon its horns shall fill,
" CRESCENT " be your motto still !

GROWING, GROWING still in HONOR,
  Still in that good men pursue ;
Honest reputation gilding
  Every gracious deed you do ;
While the Moon its horns shall fill,
" CRESCENT " be your motto still !

GROWING, GROWING still in GOODNESS,
　Drawing daily still toward Heaven;
All the emblems glowing 'round you
　For that very purpose given—
While the Moon its horns shall fill,
"CRESCENT" be your motto still!

GROWING, GROWING:—Men of "Crescent,"
　May your growing never cease,
While there is a vice to chasten,
　Or a sorrowing heart to bless!
'Till your fullness you shall see
Dawning on Eternity!

Duties of the Craft.

To afford succor to the distressed, to divide our bread with the industrious poor, and put the misguided traveler in the way, are duties of the craft, suitable to its dignity, and expressive of its usefulness.

Come and let us seek the straying,
　Lead him to the SHEPHERD back;
Come, the traveler's feet betraying,
　Guide him from the dangerous track;
Come, a solemn voice reminds us—
Come, a mystic fetter binds us—
　Masons, here your duties lie,
　Hark the poor and needy cry!

Come and help the worthy poor
　　Starving for the needed bread;
From your well-replenished store
　　Let the fellow-man be fed!
Bounties God to you supplieth
To the poor he oft denieth.

Come where sorrow has its dwelling,
　　Comfort bring to souls distressed;
To the friendless mourner telling,
　　Of the Rock that offers rest;
What would life be but for heaven?
Come, to us the WORD is given.

Band of Brothers, every nation
　　Hails your bright and orient light!
Fervent, zealous, free, your station
　　Calls for deeds of noblest might!
Seek—the world is full of sorrow—
Act—your life will end to-morrow.

———

Verdant, Fragrant, Enduring.

GREEN, but far greener is the FAITH
That gives us victory over death.
FRAGRANT, more fragrant far the HOPE
That buoys our dying spirits up.
ENDURING, but the CHARITY
That Masons teach will never die.

Fredstole: the Seat of Peace.

Far away in the West, where the savage is straying,
　　His war path all gory, his visage begrimed,
Where man hates his fellow, betrayed and betraying,
　　And nature alone breathes a spirit sublimed—
There's a FOUNTAIN whose flow sweet as nectar inviteth,
　　Embosomed in hills such as Eden adorn :—
Each sip of its waters to Friendship inciteth
　　And PEACE is the song that its song-birds return.

There met, drops the Savage his hatchet and arrow,
　　There met, breast to breast, joins in fondest embrace :
From the song-birds the foemen sweet carolings borrow,
　　And war paint the waters wash out from each face :
The hills smile around—'tis the approval of Heaven—
　　Their light catches, glances in every eye,
And speaks of a host of foul insults forgiven,
　　And pledges a Covenant that never can die.

THE LODGE is a Peace-fount! come, Brothers, and taste it!
　　O'erflowing with sweetness, to you it is given!
A ROCK its FOUNDATION—what ages have placed it!
　　Its COVERING, the starry-decked arches of Heaven.
Its LAW, 'tis inscribed in yon holiest Volume—
　　Its CHAIN, every link is the soul of a Man!
Behold on the right hand and left hand its COLUMN!
　　Behold in the East is its marvelous PLAN!

Ode for a Winter Festival.

Friends ever dear, begin the opening lay;
   Chant ye of joys that none but Masons know;
Heart answering heart, love's secret power display,
   Gain from our rites a blessing e'er we go.
      Love reigneth here—Love reigneth here;
         Hate has the rule without,
         But love reigneth here.

Bleak blows the wind : the sky with angry storms,
   Glares on the traveler as he flits along;
Here genial fire, the fire of Friendship warms,
   Here gleams the eye, here tunes the jocund song:
      Love reigneth here: Love reigneth here;
         Bleak storms may blow without,
         But Love reigneth here.

Sadness and care—our life is full of these;
   'Tis but a strife, a turmoil at the best;
Here all is calm; our walls we build in peace;
   Here one short hour the weary heart may rest.
      Love reigneth here—Love reigneth here;
         Sadness and care without,
         But love reigneth here.

The Quarry of Life.

Darkly hid beneath the quarry,
  Masons, many a true block lies;
Hands must shape and hands must carry,
  Ere the stone the Master prize.
      Seek for it—measure it—
      Fashion it—polish it!
  Then the OVERSEER will prize.

What though shapeless, rough and heavy,
  Think ye God his work will lose?
Raise the block with strength he gave ye;
  Fit it for the Master's use.
      Seek for it—measure it—
      Fashion it—polish it!
  Then the OVERSEER will use.

'Twas for this our Fathers banded—
  Through life's quarries they did roam,
Faithful-hearted, skillful-handed,
  Bearing many a true block home.
      Noticing—measuring—
      Fashioning—polishing—
  For their glorious Temple-home.

The Cedar Tree.

In the lawn that graces an aged Mason's residence, stands a Cedar Tree, planted in 1836, "for masonic purposes." Still the withered hand that placed it there to furnish sprigs of evergreen for burial use is strong enough to do THE MASTER'S WORK at each Lodge meeting, and still at an age passing the Psalmist's utmost computation, he who planted it waits patiently for the day when its limbs shall be bared of their foliage to bestrew his coffin.

Droops thy bough, oh Cedar Tree,
    Like yon dear, yon aged form—
Droops thy bough in sympathy,
    For the wreck of life's sad storm !
Sad, indeed, his weary age—
    Lonely, now, his princely home—
And the thoughts his soul engage,
    Are of winter and the tomb !

'Twas for this, oh Cedar Tree,
    Verdant midst the wintry strife,—
'Twas for this he planted thee
    Type of an immortal life—
That when round his grave in tears,
    Brothers in their ART combine,
From the store thy foliage bears,
    Each may cast a portion in !

Lo! he comes, oh Cedar Tree,
   Slowly o'er the frosted plain;
Pauses here the signs to see,
   Graven with a mystic pen!
How does each some hope express!
   Lighter gleams the wintry sky,
Lighter on his furrowed face
   Smiling at the mystery!

Soon to rest, oh Cedar Tree,
   Soon the veteran shall be borne,
There to sleep and patiently
   Wait the resurrection-morn;
Thou shalt perish from the earth;
   He in sacred youth revive,
Glorious in a better birth—
   Truths like these the emblems give.

A Lodge Valedictory.

Good-night! the spirits of the blest and good,
   From these dear walls go with you and abide;
In hours of sorrow, hours of solitude,
Or when the hosts of melancholy brood,
   And cloud your mind, may angel-spirits glide
From the WHITE THRONE and give you great delight:
   Dear friends, good-night!

Good-night! good-night! and joy be with you all;
  May sickness never blight, nor poverty;
May slanderous breath your spirits ne'er appall;
May no untoward accident befall,
  But all things prosperous and happy be;
May morning suns rise on you fresh and bright:
        Dear friends, good-night!

Good-night! and when the shadows of the grave
  Close in around you,—when the laboring breath
Draws heavily, and unto Him who gave,
You yield the spirit, be HE strong to save,
  Who is our GUIDE and SAVIOUR unto death!
Then may dear friends and heavenly hopes unite
        To say, good-night!

Hard Service, Good Wages.

Bow the back, ye Brothers, dear!—
Pinch the flesh, the work's severe!
Come, while every workman sleeps,
View the City! heaps on heaps!
See the Temple desolate!
Lo! the burnt and shattered Gate!
To repair it is your wish?—
Bow the Back! and Pinch the Flesh!

Bow the Back !—'tis hopeful toil ;
Yours the Corn and Wine and Oil,
Emblems of reward, shall be,
Plenty, Peace, and Unity !
Pinch the Flesh !—not long you wait !—
Standing in the Golden Gate,
Lo ! your Lord ! and in his hand
Wages rich at your command !

Cheer to those who, long and late,
Meet and toil at Sion's Gate !
Cheer and Courage !—See ! on high
Beams the bright ALL-SEEING EYE !
See ! the work goes bravely on ;—
Wall and Gate and Tower are won !
Grasp the Trowel !—Wield the Sword !—
Cheer !—And trust in Sion's Lord !

By the Hieroglyphics ten—
Wisdom, Strength, and Beauty's plan ;—
By the mystic Features seven—
Surely by the MASTER given :
By the Covenant-woven faith,
Strong in life, and strong in death ;—
Every hope of foeman crush !
Bow the Back ! and Pinch the Flesh !

Faith of the Olden Time.

Give me the FAITH my fathers had,
   When home-worn ties they cast,
In stern contempt forever back,
   Like chaff upon the blast.
These prayers, lip-measured, leave me chill,
As icy fount sends icy rill;
No passion bidding nature start,
No fire struck out to warm the heart;
There's nothing here to make me glad—
Give me the FAITH my fathers had.

A patriot now is bought and sold,
   For price—but render me
The hopes that braced the hearts of old,
   My fathers' LIBERTY.
What's fine-drawn speech and wordy war
A candle-ray to freedom's star!
The hand to hilt, the sword abroad,
The flag to heaven, the heart to God,
These are the tokens I would see—
Give me my fathers' LIBERTY.

Give me my fathers' walk below:
   No artful mind was theirs,
To compass kindred hearts about,
   With treachery and snares;

No nets of artifice they spread
To lure the innocent to tread;
Life's blessings how they freely shared !
Life's fear they boldly met and dared;
A blameless life, a death sublime,
These were the things of Olden Time.

Give me the friendships that entwined,
  The upright trunks of yore;
The tendrils that so sweetly vined
  A beauty and a power.
My heart is sad to think this earth,
With all its joy, with all its mirth,
Has lost the chain our fathers wove,
The chain of holy, holy love,—
Has lost the path our fathers trod,
The path that led them up to God.

Oh then bring back the palmy days,
  Of innocence and truth,
When honesty was in its prime,
  And selfishness in youth.
When man allowed to man his place,
When probity unbared its face,
When justice poised an equal scale,
And faith sang through the dying wail;
Away an age of care and crime,
Give me the days of Olden Time !

The Resurrection.

The Craft in days gone by,
Drew from their Mystery,
The mightiest truths God ever gave to men:
They whispered in the ear,
Bowed down with solemn fear,
"The dead, the buried dead shall live again!"

Oh wondrous, wondrous word!
No other Rites afford
This precious heritage, this matchless truth!
"Though gone from weeping eyes,
Though in the dust he lies,
Our Friend, our Brother, shall renew his youth!"

And we, who yet remain,
Shall meet our dead again;
Shall give the hand that thrilled within our grasp
The token of our faith,
Unchanged by time and death;—
And breast to breast his faithful form shall clasp!

But who, oh Gracious God!
The power shall afford?
Who with Omnipotence shall break the tomb?
What morning Star shall rise
To chase from sealed eyes
The long-oppressing darkness and the gloom?

Lo, at the Mystic shrine
The answer all Divine !
Lo where the Tracing-Board doth plainly tell:
"Over the horrid tomb,
The bondage and the gloom,
THE LION OF THE TRIBE OF JUDAH shall prevail!"

Then hopefully we bend
Above our sleeping friend,
And hopeful cast the green sprigs o'er his head;
'Tis but a fleeting hour—
The OMNIPOTENT hath Power,
And he will raise our Brother from the dead!

———

Consecration of a Cemetery.

In each cold bed a mortal sleeps—
    The SILENT LODGE is here!
Pale death an awful vigil keeps,
    Through all the changing year.

What tears have wet these grassy mounds!
    What sighs these winds have heard!
Oh God, have not the piteous sounds
    Thy pitying bosom stirred !

Shall man thus die and waste away
   And no fond hope be left !
Is there no sweet confiding ray
   For bosoms all bereft !

————o————

From each cold bed a form shall rise
   When the great hour shall come ;
The trump shall shake the upper skies,
   And wake the lower tomb.

No weeping then, no tear nor groan,
   For these around us spread ;
A shout shall reach the very Throne
   From the long-silent dead.

Then hush our hearts, be dry each tear,
   Wake, oh desponding faith !
And when our SAVIOUR shall appear,
   We too shall conquer death !

————o————

On these blest Graves let sunbeams pour
   Their balmiest influence ;
On them, let each reviving shower,
   Its gracious pearls dispense.

O'er these blest Graves each gentle breeze
   Its heavenly whispers breathe ;
O'er them, the foliage of the trees
   A crown of verdure wreathe.

Round these blest Graves at dead of night,
    May angel-bands combine,
And from their Mansions ever bright,
    Bring something all Divine.

————o————

From these blest Graves may hope revive;
    May JUDAH's LION tell
That we shall meet these dead alive,
    For oh, we loved them well.

Then come sad hour, we lay us down
    And calmly wait his word:
Blest are the dead, our spirits own
    Who knew and served the LORD.

————

So Mote it Be.

So MOTE IT BE with us when life shall end,
And from the East, the LORD OF LIGHT shall bend,
And we, our six days' labor fully done,
Shall claim our wages at the MASTER's throne.

So MOTE IT BE with us: that when the Square,
That perfect implement, with heavenly care,
Shall be applied to every block we bring,
No fault shall see our MASTER and our KING.

So MOTE IT BE WITH US: that though our days
Have yielded little to the MASTER's praise,
The little we have builded may be proved
To have the marks our first GRAND MASTER loved!

So MOTE IT BE WITH US: we are but weak;
Our days are few; our trials who can speak!
But sweet is our communion while we live,
And rich rewards the MASTER deigns to give.

Let's toil then, cheerfully, let's die in hope;
The WALL in wondrous grandeur riseth up;
They who come after shall the work complete,
And they and we receive the WAGES meet.

A Hebrew Chant.

Lonely is Sion, cheerless and still,
Shekinah has left thee, thou desolate Hill:
Winds sweep around thee, familiar their tone,
But trumpet, timbrel, song are gone.

Joyous was Sion on that glorious day,
When Israel beheld all thy Temple's display;
Heaven sent a token approvingly down,
But temple, altar, cloud are gone.

Foemen of Sion uplifted the spear,
The brand to thy Temple, the chains to each frere;
Pilgrims and strangers, thy children yet mourn,
But foemen, fetter, brand are gone.

Spirit of Sion, oh hasten the day,
When Israel shall gather in matchless array!
Lord! build thine altars, thy people return,
For temple, altar, cloud are gone.

Go on thy Bright Career.

Go on thy bright career, brave, faithful heart,
Prayers of the faithful every step attending;
Go spread the triumphs of the MYSTIC ART,
Wherever knee to DEITY is bending;
Raise up the landmarks, long in rubbish hidden!
Rear high the Altar on Moriah's brow;
Denounce all teachings by our rites forbidden,
And LIGHT, MORE LIGHT, on yearning hearts bestow.

Crush all things that obstruct the cause of truth;
How grand, how noble is the sacrifice!
How worthy of the brightest dreams of youth,
To build a HOUSE like that within the skies!
Oh when we lay thee, mourned-for, 'neath the sod,
And cast the green and fragrant bough of faith,
How cheerful can we give thee to thy God
Whose works defy the utmost power of death!

The Freemasons' Home.

Where hearts are warm with kindred fire,
    And love beams free from answering eyes,
Bright spirits hover always there,
    And *that's* the home the Masons prize.
        The Masons' Home! the peaceful home!
            The home of love and light and joy!
        How gladly does the Mason come
            To share his tender, sweet employ!

All round the world, by land, by sea,
    Where summers burn or winters chill,
The exiled Mason turns to thee,
    And yearns to share the joys we feel.
        The Masons' Home! the happy home!
            The home of light and love and joy!
        There's not an hour but I would come
            And share this tender, sweet employ!

A weary task, a dreary round,
    Is all benighted man may know,
But *here* a brighter scene is found,
    The brightest scene that's found below.
        The Masons' Home! the blissful home
            Glad center of unmingled joy!
        Long as I live I'll gladly come
            And share this tender, sweet employ!

And when the hour of death shall come,
And darkness seal my closing eye,
May HANDS FRATERNAL bear me home,
The home where weary Masons lie!
The Masons' Home! the heavenly home!
To faithful hearts eternal joy!
How blest to find beyond the tomb
The end of all our sweet employ!

The Dying Request.

The last request of General Morgan Lewis, Grand Master of
Masons in New York, is embodied in these lines:

The veteran sinks to rest;—
"Lay it upon my breast,
And let it crumble with my heart to dust—
Its leaves a lesson tell;—
Their verdure teacheth well
The everlasting greenness of my trust.

"Through three score years and ten,
With failing, dying men,
I've wept the uncertainties of life and time!
The symbols, loved of yore,
Have changed, have lost their power,
All save this emblem of a faith sublime.

"Things are not as they were ;—
The Level and the Square,
Those time-worn implements of love in truth,—
The incense flowing o'er—
The Lamb-skin chastely pure,
Bear not the interpretation as in youth.

"Their moral lore they lose ;
They mind me but of those
Now in death's chambers who their teachings knew ;
I see them—they but breathe
The charnel airs of death—
I cannot bear their saddening forms to view.

"But this, O symbol bright !
Surviving age's blight,
This speaks in honey-tones, unchanged, unchanged !
In it I read my youth,
In it my manhood's truth,
In it bright forms of glory long estranged.

"Green leaves of summer skies,
Blest type of Paradise !
Tokens that there's a world I soon shall see,
Of these take good supply ;
And, Brothers, when I die,
Lay them upon my breast to die with me !"

'Twas done. They're crumbled now—
He lies in ashes too;
Yet was that confidence inspired in vain?
Ah no, his noble heart,
When death's dark shades depart
With them in glory shall spring forth again.

———

The All-Seeing Eye.

There is an eye through blackest night
A vigil ever keeps;
A vision of unerring light,
O'er lowly vale, o'er giddy height,
The Eye that never sleeps.

Midst poverty and sickness lain,
The outcast lowly weeps;
What marks the face convulsed with pain?
What marks the softened look again?
The Eye that never sleeps.

Above the far meridian sun—
Below profoundest deeps,
Where dewy day his course begun,
Where scarlet marks his labor done—
The Eye that never sleeps.

No limit bounds th' Eternal Sight;
    No misty cloud o'ersweeps;
The depths of hell give up their light—
Eternity itself is bright—
    THE EYE that never sleeps.

Then rest we calm, though round our head
    The life-storm fiercely sweeps;
What fear is in the blast! what dread
In mightier Death! AN EYE's o'erhead,
    THE EYE that never sleeps.

Appreciation.

'Tis good to feel ourselves beloved of men;
To know that all our anxious cares and sighs
For others' weal is given not in vain,
But treasured up in grateful memories;
How light the toil for those we fondly love!
How rich the wages grateful spirits prove!

But when those men are BROTHERS, strongly bound
By bonds indissoluble, sweet and true;—
When gratitude springs out of sacred ground
And *prayers* are mingled with the praises due;
Ah then, toil is no burden, gifts no load!
We have full recompense for what's bestowed.

'Tis thus with you, my Friend ! the voice of all
Yields willing tribute to your high deserts ;
But from the CRAFT there comes a stronger call—
From that Great Brotherhood whose chain begirts
The broad world round, the grateful wages come
Whose price is HONOR and whose favor BLOOM.

Long may you live in Bloom and Honor, long
To show the CHRISTIAN in the MASON's guise !
In STRENGTH OMNIPOTENT may you be strong !
In WISDOM HEAVENLY may you be wise !
And when to Death's dark portals you shall come
May JESUS banish all the fear and gloom !

Leaning Towards Each Other.

The jolts of life are many,
  As we dash along the track ;
The ways are rough and rugged,
  And our bones they sorely rack.
    We're tossed about,
    We're in and out,
      We make a mighty pother—
    Far less would be
    Our pains, if we
      Would *lean* towards each other !

Behold that loving couple,
  Just mated for their life—
What care they for the joltings,
  That happy man and wife!
    The cars may jump,
    Their heads may bump,
      And jostle one another,
    They only smile,
    And try the while
      To *lean* towards each other!

Woe to the luckless pilgrim,
  Who journeys all alone!
Well said the wise King Solomon—
  "Two better is than one!"
    For when the ground's
    Most rugged found,
      And great's the pain and pother,
    He cannot break
    The sorest shake
      By *leaning* towards another!

There's not one in ten thousand,
  Of all the cares we mourn,
But what, if 'twas divided,
  Might easily be borne!
    If we'd but learn,
    When fortunes turn,

To share them with a Brother,
We'd prove how good's
Our Brotherhood,
By *leaning* towards each other !

Then, Masons, take my counsel—
The Landmarks teach you so—
Share all the joltings fairly,
As down the track you go !
Yes, give and take,
Of every shake,
With all the pain and pother,
And thus you'll prove
Your Mason's love,
By *leaning* towards each other !

The Hour of Eleven.

The expiring words of a zealous Mason were "High Eleven !"

'Twas at the hour, when laborers cast
A wistful eye to heaven,
And near the South the fervid sun
In glory shines—ELEVEN.

A skillful man with cheerful toil
His morning tasks had driven ;
He smiled to see the glowing sun
Proclaim the hour—ELEVEN.

A faithful frere, of all the band
　To him the meed was given;
'Twas not in indolence he gazed,
　Or smiled to see—ELEVEN.

His Master's work had lost no charm
　That youth and zeal had given;
Unswerving faith had buoyed him up
　From SIX to high ELEVEN.

But worn and spent, he needed rest,
　Nor could delay till even;
He felt his task was nearly done,
　And smiled to see—ELEVEN.

And soon the stroke HIGH NOON announced
　His entrance into heaven;
Prophetic proved that upward gaze,
　That smile, that word—ELEVEN.

Corn. Wine. Oil.

It is the Master's province to communicate light to the brethren.

They come from many a pleasant home—
To do the Ancient Work they come,
  With cheerful hearts and light;
They leave the world without, a space,
And gathering here in secret place,
  They spend the social night;
They earn the meed of honest toil,
Wages of CORN, and WINE, and OIL.

Upon the sacred Altar lies,
Ah many a precious sacrifice
  Made by these working men!
The passions curbed, the lusts restrained,
And hands with human gore unstained,
  And hearts from envy clean;
They earn the meed of honest toil,
Wages of CORN, and WINE, and OIL.

They do the deeds THEIR MASTER did;
The naked clothe, the hungry feed—
  They warm the shivering poor;
They wipe from fevered eyes, the tear;
A Brother's joys and griefs they share,
  As ONE had done before:
They earn the meed of honest toil,
Wages of CORN, and WINE, and OIL.

Show them how Masons Masons know,
The land of strangers journeying through,
  Show them how Masons love;
And let admiring spirits see
How reaches Masons' charity
  From earth to heaven above;
Give them the meed of honest toil,
WAGES of CORN, and WINE, and OIL.

Then will each Brother's tongue declare
How bounteous his wages are,
  And Peace will reign within;
Your walls with skillful hands will grow,
And coming generations know
  Your Temple is DIVINE;
Then give the meed of honest toil,
Wages of CORN, and WINE, and OIL.

Yes, pay these men their just desert!
Let none dissatisfied depart,
  But give them full reward;
Give LIGHT that longing eyes may see;
Give TRUTH that doth from error free;
  Give them to know the LORD!
Give them the meed of honest toil,
Wages of CORN, and WINE, and OIL.

Tribute to Robert Burns.

The sun is uprising on Scotia's far hills,
Day's labor is opening, the Grand Master wills,
But Lodge-lights are gleaming in cheerfulness yet,
Afar in the west, where we Masons are met.
There's song for the tuneful, kind words for the kind,
There's cheer for the social, and light for the blind,
But when we, uprising, prepare us to go,
With one thought and feeling we'll sing thy ADIEU.

A melting farewell to the favored and bright,—
A sorrowful thought for the sun set in night,—
A round to the Bard whom misfortunes befell,—
A prayer that his spirit with Masons may dwell.
When freedom and harmony bless our design,
We'll think of thee, Brother, who loved every line;
And when gloomy clouds shall our Temple enshroud,
The voice of thy music shall come from the cloud.

Across the broad ocean two hands shall unite,
Columbia,—Scotia,—the symbol is bright!
The world one Grand Lodge, and the heaven above,
Shall witness the triumph of Faith, Hope, and Love;
And thou, sweetest Bard, when our gems we enshrine,
Thy jewel, the brightest, most precious, shall shine,
Shall gleam from the East, to the far distant West,
While morning shall call us, or evening shall rest.

The Foundation Stone.

When the SPIRIT came to Jephthah,
  Animating his great heart,
He arose, put on his armor,
  Girt his loins about to part,
Bowed the knee, implored a blessing,
  Gave an earnest of his faith,
Then, divinely-strung, departed,
  Set for victory or death.

If a rude, uncultured soldier
  Thus drew Wisdom from above,
How should we, enlightened Laborers,
  Children of the Sire of Love,—
How should we, who know "the Wisdom
  Gentle, pure and peaceable,"
Make a prayerful preparation
  That our work be square and full!

Lo the future! ONE can read it—
  HE its darkest chance can bend:
Lo our wants, how great, how many!
  HE abundant means can lend:
Raise your hearts then, Pilgrims, boldly
  Build and journey in his trust:
Square your deeds by precepts holy,
  And the end is surely blest.

Vainly will the builders labor
  If the OVERSEER is gone;
Vainly gate and wall are guarded
  If the ALL-SEEING is withdrawn;
Only is successful ending
  When the work's begun with care;
Lay your blocks, then, Laborers, strongly,
  On the Eternal Rock of Prayer.

———

The Inheritance of Friendship.

When twenty years have circled round,
  The lads now standing at my knee
Will cherish one poor spot of ground
  Sacred to memory and me.
    Gazing upon the humble sod,
    Recalling each fond, loving word,
    They'll keep one link in memory's chain
    Bright, till the hour we meet again.

Such is the lesson I impart
  At evening's set when prayers are said:
The last sweet sentiment at heart
  Ere little eyes are closed in bed.
    That when upon life's billows tossed,
    In worldly selfishness engrossed,
    A CABLE-TOW the thought shall prove
    To draw them by a Father's love.

When twenty years have come and gone
  They who shall fondly look for you
Must leave the scenes you now adorn
  And seek the sodded hillock too:
    Tears will bedew the grass beneath,
    Sighs will unite with nature's breath,
    To embalm within that hallowed bed,
    A father loved, a father dead.

There's Brotherhood in honest sighs,
  There's Brotherhood in earnest tears:
Our sons, made kindred by such ties,
  Shall interchange their hopes and fears:
    Yours to the WEST their steps will bend
    To honor their dear Father's friend:
    Mine to the EAST will make their way
    A pious pilgrimage to pay.

Such was the dream that fired my brain
  Last night as mid my loved ones lying,
It came again, again, again,
  And traced itself in lines undying.
    I dreamed we twain had joined the bands
    Who live and love in other lands,
    And from high seats beheld with joy
    The step of each dear pilgrim-boy.

I dreamed that on some sunny plain
　　They, o'er whose couch we've bent at night,
Met, twined with eager hands the chain,
　　The Chain of Love, the Chain of Light;
　　　　With glowing lips exchanged the Word—
　　　　No fonder does our tongue afford,—
　　　　And Covenanted by that faith
　　　　Their fathers pledged and kept till death.

Then be it so, dear Friend, and while
　　For earthly labors we are spared,
Let's teach our sons to cherish well
　　The friendship we've so freely shared.
　　　　Then at life's sunset we may die
　　　　And yet the power of Death defy:
　　　　Then by the Monster-victor slain
　　　　In our dear Children live again!

———

To Masons Everywhere.

In gladsome mood again we're met—
　　How swiftly passed the year!
Begin the feast, and, Brothers, drink
　　To Masons everywhere!
　　　　A Mason's love is unrestrained;
　　　　Each other's woes we share;
　　　　Then lift the cup, and, Brothers, drink
　　　　To Masons everywhere!

What would our Mystic Tie be worth—
  How little should we care
For Masonry, did not its links
  Encircle everywhere !
    With Masons' love so unrestrained,
      Each other's woes to share,
    Well may we fill the cup and drink
      To Masons everywhere !

Though some we loved have fallen on
  The weary path of care,
What then ! in heaven they're yet our own !
  To Masons everywhere !
    For Masons' love, so unrestrained,
      Eternity may dare !
    Then, Brothers, fill, and fondly drink
      To Masons everywhere !

And so, when death shall claim us, too,
  And other forms be here,
May we in memory's heart be held
  By Masons everywhere !
    For Masons' love is unrestrained,
      Nor death the chain may tear;
    O'erflow the cup, and, Brothers, drink
      To Masons everywhere !

A Masonic Greeting.

Lo, from the distant West,
Lo, from your honored guest
The voice of greeting and a word of prayer;
Ye Sons of Cheer, all hail!
This grateful tongue shall tell
The tie that binds you and the joys you share!

There is a CORD of length,
There is a CHAIN of strength,
Around you each I see the sacred coil;
How long, ah, well I know!
How strong, your deeds do show,
The while you labor in the sacred toil.

In amplest share bestowed,
By Him you worship—GOD,
The joy of Friendship well you feel and prize,
'Tis HIS own best design,
'Tis perfect, 'tis divine,
It is the bliss diffused through upper skies.

Peace be within your halls!
The CEMENT of your walls
Be HOLY LOVE—pure, indestructible!
From the o'erarching Heaven
A gracious smile be given,
The favor of a DEITY to tell!

When each shall bow in death,
Joy to the parting breath !
Rich fragrance from a thousand generous deeds !
And where your ashes be,
Sacred to memory
The spot while man pure truth and honor heeds !

And me, oh loving Friends,
When life's poor story ends,
Me in your inner heart of hearts enshrine !
Humble, but oh sincere,—
Erring and sorrowing here,
Write me as one who loved each Mystic line !

Builders of light, your hands !
Distant our several lands ?
No ; for I see, I hear, I feel you now !
Bind once again the chain ;
Again, dear Friends, again ;
Hear, Gracious Lord, hear and confirm the Vow !

The Happy Hour.

Oh happy hour when Masons meet !
Oh rarest joys that Masons greet !
Each interwoven with the other,
And Brother truly joined with Brother,
In intercourse that none can daunt,
Linked by the ties of COVENANT.

See, ranged about the Holy Word,
The Craftsmen praise their common LORD !
See in each eye a love well proven !
Around each heart a faith well woven !
Feel, in each hand-grip, what a tie
Is this whose scope is MASONRY.

Blest bond ! when broken, we would fain
Unite the severed links again ;
Would urge the tardy hours along,
To spend the wealth of light and song,
That makes the Lodge a sacred spot ;
Oh, be the season ne'er forgot,
That takes us from a world of care
To happy scenes where Masons are !

The World-wide Recognition.

Wherever man is tracing
    The weary ways of care,
'Midst wild and desert pacing,
    Or lands of softer air,
WE SURELY KNOW EACH OTHER,
    And with true words of cheer,
Each Brother hails his Brother,
    And hope wings lightly there.

Wherever tears are falling—
  The soul's dark wintry rain—
And human sighs are calling
  To human hearts in vain,
We surely know each other, etc.

Wherever prayer is spoken,
  In earnestness of Faith,
We're minded of the TOKEN
  That tells our Master's death.
We pray, then, for each other, etc.

Wherever man is lying
  Unknowing and unknown,
There's one yet by the dying—
  He shall not die alone.
For then we know each other, etc.

The Widow and the Fatherless.

As on my road delaying,
  The stream's cool waters by,
My thoughts in fancy straying,
  I heard a plaintive cry:
"There may be hope in heaven—
  For *us* no hope is here;
Oh, why was joy thus given,
  So soon to disappear!"

Around the grave was weeping
A widowed, orphaned band;
Beneath their feet was sleeping
The husband, father, friend;
And as their sorrows, swelling,
Broke forth midst sigh and tear,
Again these words were telling—
"Alas, no hope is here!"

The stream's cool waters flowing,
No longer sung to me—
The soft spring sunbeams glowing,
Were cheerless all to see;
For still that widowed mother,
And still those orphans dear,
Bewailed my buried BROTHER—
"Alas, no hope is here!"

MY BROTHER? yes, forsaken,
These lov'd ones round thee mourn;
Too soon from friendship taken,
Dear Brother, thou art gone!
Gone from a cold world's sighing,
From sorrow and from fear,
But left these mourners crying—
"Alas, no hope is here!"

Those tears, my heart, are holy !
   Those sighs by anguish driven,
This mourning group so lowly,
   Are messengers of Heaven;
And so will I receive them,
   As God shall give me cheer,
Protect them and relieve them,
   And teach them HOPE IS HERE !

—————

The Death of the Grand Master.

CRAWFORD, Grand Master of Maryland, died under the affecting
circumstances here described:

His voice was low, his utterance choked,
   He seemed like one in sorrow bound,
As from the ORIENT he invoked
   God's blessings on the Masons round.

'Tis sad to see the strong man weep—
   Tears are for sorrows yet untried ;
But who his sympathy can keep,
   When age unseals emotion's tide ?

Reverently stood the Brothers round,
   While their Grand Master breathed farewell,
And strove to catch the faintest sound
   Of accents known and loved so well.

He told them of the zealous care
 Of their forefathers of the ART;
How valley-gloom and mountain-air
 Bore witness of the faithful heart.

He conned the precepts, line by line—
 Oh, that the Craft may ne'er despise
Precepts so precious, so divine,
 That shape the Mason-mysteries.

He warned them of a world unkind,
 Harsh to the good, to evil mild,
Whose surest messengers are blind,
 Whose purest fountains are defiled.

He told them of a world to come,
 To which this life a portal is,
Where tired laborers go home,
 To scenes of never-ending bliss.

Then of himself he humbly spoke—
 So modestly! so tenderly!
While from the saddened group there broke
 An answering sigh of sympathy:

"Now give me rest: my years demand
 A holiday, Companions dear!
My days are drawing to an end,
 And I would for my end prepare.

"Now give me rest; but when you meet,
  Brothers, in this beloved spot,
My name upon your lips repeat,
  And never let it be forgot!

"Now unto GOD, the Masons' FRIEND,
  The GOD our emblems brightly tell,
Your dearest interests I commend—
  Brothers, dear Brothers, oh, farewell!"

Down from the Orient, slowly down,
  Weeping, through that sad group he passed,
Turned once and gazed, and then was gone—
  That look—his tenderest and his last.

His last—for, ere the week had sped,
  That group, with sorrow unrepressed,
Gathered around their honored dead—
  Bore their Grand Master to his rest!

The Veteran's Lament.

There's tenfold Lodges in the land
  Than when my days were few;
But none can number such a band,
  The wise, the bright, the true,
As stood around me on the night,
When first I saw the MYSTIC LIGHT,
  Full fifty years ago.

There's Brother love and Brother aid,
   Where'er the Craft is known;
But none like that whose twinings made
   The mighty chain that's gone—
Ah, none like that which bound my soul
When first my eyes beheld the goal
     Full fifty years ago.

There's emblems green to deck the bed
   Of Masons where they rest,
But none like those we used to spread
   Upon the Mason's breast,
When, yielding up to death, they fell,
Who'd battled with the monster well,
     Full fifty years ago.

Oh, how my heart is kindled now,
   When round me meet again
The shadows of the noble few,
   Who formed the mystic train
In which my feet were proud to tread,
When through admiring crowds we sped,
     Full fifty years ago.

They're fled, that noble train,—they're gone,—
   Their last procession's o'er,—
And I am left to brood alone,
   Ere I, too, leave the shore;

But while I have a grateful tear,
I'll praise the bright ones that were here,
Full fifty years ago.

———

Washington.

" Glory to God, in courts of glory high !
  Earth, balmy peace! good will, good will to men !"
O'er the still plain, beneath the Christmas sky
  Ring the glad tidings; and again, again,
" Glory to God, to God !" the dewy plain
  Echoes the notes; the midnight solitude,
Wood, mount, and waters, catch the glowing strain !
  Ah, ne'er was heard such note since Satan stood,
  Sad hour, in Eden's groves, and worked to man no good!

Heaven's joy that night was perfect ! CHRIST was born!
  IMMANUEL, PRINCE OF PEACE, and SON OF GOD !
New grief to demons, wailing and forlorn,
  Pierced through their souls as an envenomed sword
" To God, to God on high !"—thus the accord—
  " On Earth good will and peace, good will and peace !"
Now far ascending, singing as they soared,
  The angelic sisters vanish; echoes cease,
  And, from their mystic trance, the Shepherds' souls
    release.

Spirits of peace, since that bright Christmas eve,
    Have oft descended from the ladder's top,
And brought to those who suffer and believe
    The priceless blessings of the Christian's hope—
That soon humanity will cease to grope
    In doubts and darkness, as in days gone by,
And follow HIM, the PEACEFUL, journeying up,
    From Bethlehem to gory Calvary,
    Who died that we might live, and lives eternally.

Heaven sent a Washington! there was much need—
    Ages had rolled along, and hearts had bled
And liberty, down-trodden as a weed,
    No shelter found for her defenceless head :
Peace lay, like Lazarus, in sepulchral bed :—
    God raised up Washington, and freedom smiled !
Once more to yearning hearts the angels said,
    " Good will to man, of grace the favored child !
    " Good will to man !" that voice shall never more be stilled.

On TRESTLE-BOARD DIVINE the plan was traced—
    The MASTER ARCHITECT his work surveyed ;
Each virtue in its proper balance placed ;
    Each ornament of purest metal made ;
Each block in symmetry exact was laid ;
    And there stood Washington, the Mason-man !
Wise unto warfare's sanguinary trade,
    Wiser to PEACE—such was the MASTER's plan,
    And Wisdom, Beauty, Strength, through all the Temple ran !

Caution his chiefest care; the outer gate
  Was strictly guarded; through its portals came
Nought that betrayed; prudent, deliberate,
  Each messenger bore out undoubted claim
To instant reverence and deathless fame.
  Thus, tyled with care, his sanctuary kept,
Unstained its altar, unforgot its flame,
  While sentinels on other watch-towers slept,
  And *Prudence* o'er the ills of sad indifference wept.

Sober in all things—*Temperance*, the spring
  Of human strength, was paramount in him;
There was no vile excess or lust to bring
  Untimely feebleness to manly limb,
Or dull his ear, or make his eye grow dim.
  Like one of old, the Leader through the sea,
Floated no changes on life's rapid stream;
  Age brought him death, but not infirmity—
  Bore hence the vigorous frame, unshaken by decay.

How great his *Fortitude!* protracted war
  Caused patriot hearts to sink dispirited;
His bleeding army cast in flight before
  A taunting enemy; his hopes betrayed—
How great his *Fortitude!* firm, undismayed,
  The pillar of his suffering country stood,
By night a glow, by day refreshing shade,
  A column fixed, unshaken, unsubdued!
  Plumbed by the Master's hand, by him pronouncèd Good!

Excellent he in *Justice ;* if to do,
 In all that life presents, from day to day,
To others as you would they do to you,—
 If this be Masonry, a Mason he !
Unswerving to the right or left, his way
 Was *onward, upward ;* in his hand the scale
Of righteousness was equipoised, to pay
 Homage to God—hail, Great Creator, hail !
Justice to man—for man was *Brother* cherished well.

But not these sterner virtues only stand
 Around this good man's life ; true *Brotherly Love,*
Such as the ancient brethren cherished, and
 Relief that does both pain and woe remove,
And *Truth,* an attribute of God above,
 Clustered like dropping vines on Washington.
What marvel that admiring Masons strove
 To catch the light from such a matchless sun,
 Or claim the mantle, ere the godlike chief was gone !

Henceforth the Christmas song need not be stilled !
 The conqueror, ere the battle's turmoil cease,
Turns from the glory of the encrimsoned field
 And bends in homage to the Prince of Peace.
" Glory to God "—that anthem shall increase,
 " On Earth " such lives proclaim " Good will to man ! "
Henceforth, when angels sing Immanuel's grace,
 We'll strike the harp, and recognize the plan ;
 Oh, that our earth might yield such Temple-work again *!*

Lo the sands swiftly run ! behold, our lives
 Dropping, like foliage, to a solemn close !
To-day the bud bright expectation gives,
 To-morrow blossoms to a transient rose ;
Another morn, and its whole beauty goes ;
 Its leaves are scattered wastefully around,
No heart remembering ; another glows
 Upon the stem ; another hope is crowned ;
 And this is human life, the life the dead have found.

Count well the moments then, fill up the day !
 Brothers, let wisdom's hand your life-plans trace !
The Temple will be finished, though we may
 Not see the STONE exalted to its place :
It is enough that God will see and bless :
 Labor while it is day ; there's work for all ;
The TRESTLE-BOARD proclaims it, and alas !
 Too soon will night spread round its hueless pall :
 Too soon *the grave, the grave* from which there's no recall.

Clouds may obscure us ; slander may detract ;
 The foes of truth and rectitude unite ;
But while within our mystic sphere we act,
 There lives no power can hinder or affright.
The Master's eye still oversees the right ;
 Heaven's books record it with angelic pen ;
And when death's summons calls us up the height,
 A full reward for labor shall we gain,
 In God's own Temple freed from sorrow, toil and pain.

Man of a thousand virtues, Washington!
 Thy model, lent from heaven, we prefer;
Our deeds, upon that high design begun,
 Shall merit praise, tried by the CHIEF O'ERSEER:
Master of men! hear thou the Mason's prayer!
 Breathe in our spirits a true love of peace;
Teach us a brother's bonds and woes to share;
 Enlarge our charity, our faith increase,
And save us all in CHRIST, the Mason's Righteousness!

The Three Salutes.

I hail you, Brother, in the place
 Where none but those should meet
Whose *types* are bended knee and brow,
 And the uncovered feet;
I take you by the grip, expressing
 All that heart can feel,
And I pledge myself to be to you,
 A Brother TRUE AS STEEL!

I've watched with real joy your quest,
 So ardent and so rare—
Your bold, unflinching gaze upon
 The things we most revere;
I've seen that nothing daunts you
 In the paths our LIGHTS reveal;
And I pledge myself again to you,
 A Brother TRUE AS STEEL!

I think there's that within you
    Only needs for *time* to show—
Will kindle up a flame where
    Others only feel a *glow ;*
I think the grave will claim you,
    As a Mason ripe and leal ;
And so once more I pledge myself
    A Brother TRUE AS STEEL !

The Master of the Upright Heart.

German authors describe the affecting incident given in the following lines.   The opening verses allude to a journey up the Mississippi
river in 1853, swollen at that time out of its banks, during which the
author related the incident to his children.

We journeyed up the Western flood,
    My little boys and I,
And watched the drifts of ice and wood
    That floated swiftly by ;
While banks and trees and dwellings too
Appeared like islands in the view.

We marked with sympathy and grief
    The general distress,
And fain the lads would give relief
    To every suffering case ;—
But when a corpse came floating past
They fled the spectacle aghast.

Then in our little room we met
  Each on a willing knee
And listened to the various fate
  Of men by land and sea;
Of shipwrecked sailors starved for food
And lost ones wandering in the wood.

I told them of such noble deeds
  Where rescue had been given,
Such generous acts, that he who reads
  Is moved to worship heaven.
But most I pleased them with the part
Of Julian of " The Upright Heart."

" 'Twas on a stormy April day,
  The floods were at their height,
All Frankfort gather'd out, they say,
  To see a dismal sight.
A broken bridge—a swollen sea—
And oh, a drowning family !

" The Master of ' The Upright Heart '
  Was Frankfort's noblest son:
On many a field of high desert
  His laurels had been won,
Not laurels wet with human blood
But those acceptable to God.

"Smiles from the face of cold despair,—
   The widow's grateful song—
The orphan's praise—the stranger's prayer—
   These to his crown belong;
Ah! many such, thank God, there be
In our world-wide fraternity!

"Prince Julian galloped to the brink
   Of that tremendous flood;
The perishing about to sink
   Inspired his noble blood.
He called aloud, he called the brave
This wretched family to save!

"None answered him; again he cried:
   'Oh! have you hearts of stone,
To see them perish by your side?
   Look! look! they wave us on!'
He offered gold as water free,
To save the drowning family!

"But when the boldest shrunk—deterred
   From such a desperate deed—
He uttered not another word;
   He bowed his pious head,
Looked upwards—gave his soul to God—
And plunged into the raging flood!

"That day the gates of Heaven were thrown
  To admit a spirit freed;
That day earth lost its noblest son,
  And gave him to the dead;
That day enshrined the Royal Art,
Her hero of 'The Upright Heart!'"

The lads sat thoughtful on my knee,
  Reflecting on the tale;
They loved to talk of Masonry,
  And knew its precepts well;
"*I know what made him take such pains;
The signs they made were Mason's signs!*"

Masonic Valedictory.

When auld acquaintance closing round,
  Their parting grips entwine;
What song awakes the tender sigh,
  Like auld lang syne!
  'Tis auld lang syne, the voice
  Of other days divine!
Come, Brothers, now a parting word
  To auld lang syne.

From many a pilgrim-pathway come,
  To work the grand design.
We've wrought, and praised the sacred bond
  Of auld lang syne.
  Of auld lang syne, the bond
  Of auld lang syne
Our fathers marked the sacred way
  In auld lang syne.

Though wintry blasts the flesh may chill,
  Though torrid suns may shine,
Our hearts' response unchanged will beat
  To auld lang syne.
  To auld lang syne, they beat
  To auld lang syne;
Each pulse responsive, thrilling high,
  To auld lang syne.

Adieu, adieu! the falling tear
  To friendship we assign;
Your hand, your hand, my brother dear,
  For auld lang syne!
  For auld lang syne, adieu
  For auld lang syne.
Ah! rent forever is the bond
  Of auld lang syne.

A Masonic Symposium.

At a New Year's Eve Festival at Chicago, Illinois, 1862–'3, twenty-eight Masons sat the Old Year out and the New Year in. To commemorate the pleasant event, a "Memorial" of songs was published, of which the following was the Exordium.

(The Craft Assemble in Merry Mood.)

High carnival to-night: a year of gloom,
   A twelvemonth, murky with the fogs of war,
Has ended; all its wrecks and ruin done;
   Its severed bonds; its Lodges, closed and still:
Its altars overthrown; its jewels soiled;
   Its lambskins spotted with the hue of blood;—
The tale of horror, to its latest page,
   Is done, and FINIS written at the close.

High carnival to-night: a genial band,
   About refreshments' Altar circled close,
Brings each his sacrifice and lays thereon:
   Each brings his jest, and each a merry thought,
   And his kind eyes that speak unuttered love.

High carnival to-night; pass round the quip—
Let not the fire of wit go down, nor give
One moment to the saddening reign of care.
No GAVEL here; no frowning face; no voice
Of MASTER to subdue the craftsmen's joys.
'Tis the last night, last hour of '62,
And we will drown it in a flood of mirth.

(The Signal of Low XII. is heard.)

But lo, the clock, 'tis midnight! stealthy feet
Of murderers creeping by, fall on the ear,
And smothered voices whisper wonted words.
'Tis midnight! quick, ye mystic crew, come round—
Close in, strong men, impenetrable lines,
And weave the INDISSOLUBLE CHAIN OF LOVE.

(The Midnight Song of Masons.)

Sing now departed joys; sing high, ye Craft,
Whose solemn march is ever timed to song;
Sing ye of days, ah never to return!
Of friends forever parted: sing, with tears,
Of those, beneath th' Acacia sprigs that sleep,
And let the last stroke of the parted year
Be holy with remembrance of their love.

(Hail to the New Year.)

Huzza, sing louder now! strain every voice
In honor of the YEAR, the new-born YEAR,
The blessed, hopeful, happy '63!
Of all its health, and wealth, and bliss, sing high!
Of wives' love and of children's, blessed love,
Of friends and friendship, everything that God
Can yield on earth to His most favored ones.

(The Prospective View.)

Twelve teeming months lie spread before our eyes;
Cease now to sing, and contemplate their train:
EACH MONTH a treasure from the Gracious Hand,
Of means and rich occasions to do good.
Join silently in RESOLUTION now,
And, Brothers, say, shall we not, through this year,
Live nearer to our duty? walk more true
To PLUMB-LINE and to SQUARE than in the past?
Shall not our COVENANTS join, in closer bond,
Us to each other and the whole to God?

The Narrow Boundary.

So each one stands—a narrow line
    Divides the future from the past—
A little space to labor in,
    Too brief for purposes so vast.

Those grand designs, whose tracing proves
    Our inspiration is from heaven—
Those boundless hopes—those deathless loves—
    'Tis but a day to these is given!

Then let us labor while we can—
    Throw off the burdens that oppress—
Redeem this poor and fleeting span
    And look to God to help and bless!

And should we seek, to give us cheer,
  Examples of the bold and true,
A cloud of witnesses is here
  To prove what laboring men can do.

———

New Year's Reflections.

Shall we see it, loving Brothers,
  Ere another New Year's day ?
Shall we join those loving others
  Whom the past year tore away ?
    Shall we change this toil and drudge,
    For the bright CELESTIAL LODGE,
      T. C. L. A. W.
      T. S. A. O. T. U. P.?

Shall we tread that one more station,
  Take that last and best degree
Whose consummate "Preparation"
  Is *to set the spirit free?*
    Lay our bodies off that then
    Souls unburdened may go in,
      T. C. L. A. W.
      T. S. A. O. T. U. P.?

Shall we find beyond the river—
  Shall we find beyond the tomb,
Those who left us, not forever,
  Left us till we too should come ?
    Shall we learn the long-lost WORD
    That admits a man to GOD—
        T. C. L. A. W.
        T. S. A. O. T. U. P. ?

Then, be zealous, loving Brothers,
  While your lives so swiftly tend;
Emulate those faithful others
  In the prizes they have gained;
    O'er the river, on the shore,
    They are happy evermore,
        T. C. L. A. W.
        T. S. A. O. T. U. P.

Toil,—your wages rich are ready;
  Bear,—your burdens all shall cease;
Give,—however poor and needy;
  Pray,—and God will give release
    From this bitter toil and drudge
    To the bright CELESTIAL LODGE,
        T. C. L. A. W.
        T. S. A. O. T. U. P. !

Timely Warning.

We whisper good counsel in the ear of a Brother, and, in the most tender manner, remind him of his faults and endeavor to aid his reformation.

Where is thy Brother, Craftsman, say,
Where is the erring one to-day ?
We look around the festive band,—
What cheerful smiles on every hand !
The voice of laughter swells amain—
Where is the brightest of the train ?
The ready wit, the generous word,
The glee in music's best accord,
The bounteous gifts—oh where is he,
The prince of Mason's revelry ?
Not left unwarned in death to fall ?
To lapse without one friendly call ?

Alas, the grave has closed above
So many objects of our love !
There is so many a vacant chair
In every group where Masons are !
Of some the drunkard's cup doth tell ;
Tempted, yet sorrowing *they fell ;*
Day after day they saw the light
Recede, till day was turned to night ;
Yet yearned and strove to pause, and stay
Their feet upon the slippery way ;
They fell, and none so bright are left
As those of whom we are bereft.

A voice from out the grave demands—
" Where is thy Brother ? are thy hands,
Quite guiltless of his priceless blood ?
How often have ye kindly stood,
And whispered loving word and prayer,
Within the erring Brother's ear ?
How often counseled, plead, and warned,
And from approaching danger turned ? "
The thoughtful tear, the heavy sigh,
Must speak for conscience a reply:
Quick then, oh Craftsman, up and save
The living from untimely grave !

A Welcome into Masonry.

Directed to one who subsequently acquired a distinguished name
as a Masonic writer.

There were many with me were glad, Brother,
  When we read your later thought,
And to one another we said, Brother,
  'Tis an omen of good import !
For the battle of law has begun, Brother,
  The strife for " the good old way,"
And we need just such an one, Brother,
  As we knew you of old to be !

Yes, one of the daring type, Brother—
    Such men as they had of yore,
With a head that in age is ripe, Brother,
    And a heart that is brimming o'er ;
To know what a LANDMARK is, Brother—
    In love to be warm and true—
Oh, how have we longed for these, Brother,
    And 'tis these we shall find in you !

In the day when your sands are spent, Brother,
    And the Craft shall your history tell,
They'll say, as their grief has vent, Brother,
    "He has done his labor well !"
For you know we have ARCHIVES, Brother,
    And a COLUMN rent in twain,
And a NAME that still greenly lives, Brother,
    Though the dust hath its dust again !

And these they'll give to you, Brother,
    As the guerdon of your meed ;
For the love that is warm and true, Brother,
    For the heart and for the head ;
For the battle of law has begun, Brother,
    The strife for "the good old way,"
And we need just such an one as you, Brother,
    As we know you of old to be !

Dividing the Tessera.

The ancient practice of sealing a devoted friendship between parting friends, by separating some metallic substance, as a ring, a coin and the like, and dividing the fragments between the parties, is not altogether disused. In the rural districts of England and Scotland it is a custom of lovers, and many a poor laborer whose body lies buried in the soil of the Western Continent, bore upon his person at his dying hour this token of betrothal with one who shall never again meet him on earth.

As a Masonic practice, we could wish it were more common. It is ancient, more ancient than any other manner of expressing friendship at parting. It is suitable to the symbolical character of our lessons. To rescue it from its present position as a mere amatory token, were worthy of our most accomplished writers.

The following verses relate to an incident in the history of two orphan youth, adopted and educated by a benevolent widow in New Jersey. They became Masons at the same communication, were deeply indoctrinated in the symbolic beauties of the Royal Art, and, when they parted to pursue different fortunes—one to fill an honorable post in the army in Mexico, the other an officer on board an India Merchantman—they divided *a golden ring* between them, as a Tessera, and each suspended a portion nearest his heart. They never met again. They, of whom it had been said, as of the early Christians, that "they possessed all things in common," fill graves as widely separated as the east is from the west. The lady whose charity gave them education, and the opportunity for usefulness and distinction, has now in her possession both the *golden fragments*, sent her with dying messages—the one from Vera Cruz, the other from Ceylon.

> Parting on the sounding shore
>
> Brothers twain were sighing;
>
> Mingle with the ocean's roar,
>
> Words of love undying;
>
> A ring of gold was severed then
>
> And each to each the giver,
>
> His faith renewed in mystic sign
>
> And bound his heart forever.

138

"Broken thus THE TOKEN be,
    While o'er earth we wander;
One to thee and one to me—
    Rudely torn asunder;
But though divided we are one—
    This scar the bond expresses,
When all our painful wandering's done,
    Will close and leave no traces!

" Warmly in thy bosom hide,
    The golden voice, *I love thee !*
Keep it there whate'er betide,
    To guard thee and to prove thee !
And should THE TOKEN e'er be lost,
    Or chilled, what now is riven,
I'll know that death has sent the frost
    And look for thee in heaven !"

Parted on the sounding shore,
    Each THE TOKEN keeping,
Met those Brothers never more—
    In death they're widely sleeping.
But yet love's victory was won,—
    The scar that bond expresses,—
Their long and painful wandering's done—
    Hath closed and left no traces!

High XII.

The custom of lodge-refreshment, time-honored and sanctioned by the example of the noblest and best of American Masons, might well be renewed. The Order with us has too much of the pulpit and too little of the table. A due intermixture of both was what the Craft in the olden time regarded.

There's Pillars II. and Columns V.
Support and grace our halls of truth,
But none such sparkling pleasure give
As the Column that adorns the S'.
"High XII." the Junior Warden calls—
His Column grants the festive hour,
And through our antiquated halls,
Rich streams of social gladness pour.

'Tis then, all toil and care forgot,
The Bond *indissoluble* seems:
'Tis then the world's a happy spot,
And hope, unmixed with sadness, gleams.
High XII.: I've shared the festive hour
With those who realize the bliss,
And felt that life contains no more
Than sparkles in the joys of this.

What memories hover round the time!
What forms rise up to call it blest!
Departed Friends: why should it dim
Our joys to know that they're at rest!

HIGH XII. ! how they rejoiced to hear !
   Quickly each implement laid down,
   Glad to exchange for toil and care
    And heavy CROSS, a heavenly CROWN !

The Comrades all, by 3 × 3,
   Linked in the golden chain of Truth,
A hearty welcome pledge with me
   To the Column that adorns the S' !
    HIGH XII. : and never be the hour
     Less free, less brotherly than now !
    HIGH XII. : a rich libation pour
     To joys that none but Masons know !

The Checkered Pavement.

There is no emblem teaches a more practical every-day lesson to a Freemason than the Mosaic pavement, denoting human life checkered with good and evil.

I, on the WHITE SQUARE, *you* on the BLACK ;
I at fortune's *face*, *you* at her *back ;*
Friends to *me many*, friends to *you few ;*
What, then, dear Brother, binds me to you ?
   This, THE GREAT COVENANT in which we abide—
    HEARTS charged with sympathy—
     HANDS opened wide—
    LIPS filled with comfort,
     And GOD to provide.

I, in life's *valley, you* on its *crest ;*
I at its *lowest, you* at its *best ;*
I sick and sorrowing, you hale and free ;
What, then, dear Brother, binds you to me ?
 This, THE GREAT COVENANT in which we abide—
  HEARTS charged with sympathy—
  HANDS opened wide—
  LIPS filled with comfort,
  And GOD to provide.

They in death's slumber, *we* yet alive ;
They freed from labor, *we* yet to strive ;
They paid and joyful, *we* tired and sad—
What, then, to us, Brother, bindeth the *dead ?*
 This, THE GREAT COVENANT in which we abide—
  HEARTS charged with sympathy—
  HANDS opened wide—
  LIPS filled with comfort,
  And GOD to provide.

Let none be comfortless, let none despair ;
Lo round the *Black* grouped the *White Ashlars* are !
Stand by each other, black fortune defy,
All these vicissitudes end by and by.
 Keep THE GREAT COVENANT wherein we abide—
  "HEARTS charged with sympathy—
  HANDS opened wide—
  LIPS filled with comfort,
  And GOD *will* provide !"

The Focus of the Lodge.

It is admitted by lecturers and Masonic speakers, that the true acoustical focus of the lodge is near the Northeast corner. This is attributed to the fact that it was there each of us received those first impressions on which to build our future moral and masonic edifice. Certainly in no other part of the room can the speaker give utterance, so truly and eloquently, to the genuine sentiments of the Order; and the unhappy debates which sometimes disturb the harmony of our meetings, would be obviated were speakers required to take their stand at the focus of the lodge!

Oh, when before the lodge we stand,
 Its walls hung round with mystic lines,
And for the loving, listening band,
 Draw truth and light from those designs;—
See ON THE RIGHT, the Open Word,
 Which lendeth grace to every thought!
See ON THE LEFT, the Mason's lord!
 'Tis chosen well, the sacred spot!

For there our youthful minds received
 The earliest impress of that light,
Whose perfect radiance, believed,
 Will lead the soul to Heavenly height.
Around the spot there clusters much
 Of Masons' lore; and dull were he
Who, standing in the light of such,
 Cannot unveil our Mystery.

If in Instruction's voice there come
   A tone of hatred, if, alas,
The love and music of our home
   Be changed to discord and disgrace,—
'Tis that the speaker has forgot
   The solemn words first uttered there,—
His feet have left the sacred spot,
   His heart and tongue no wisdom bear.

But when the soul is kindled high,
   With love, such love as angels know—
And when the tongue trips lightly by
   The truth and love our emblems show ;—
When round the lodge, the eye and cheek
   Prove how congenial is the theme,
No further need the speaker seek—
   Good spirits stand and speak with him !

The Decayed Lodge.

These walls are tottering to decay;
   There's dampness on the stair;
But well I mind me of the day
   When two-score men met here :
When two-score brothers met at night,
   The full round Moon above,
To weave the mystic chain of light
   With holy links of love.

But now the lightest of the train,
  In early grave is bowed;
The chain is broke, the holy chain—
  The MASTER's with his GOD!
The wailing notes were heard one day,
  Where cheerful songs are best,
And two-score Brothers bore away
  Their MASTER to his rest.

The SOUTH, that pleasant voice, is still,
  That spoke the joys of noon;
The WEST, that told the Master's will,
  Has set as sets the sun.
The sun may rise, may stand, may fall,
  But these will stand no more—
No more the faithful craft to call,
  Or scan their labors o'er.

I'll weep the rending of this chain,
  As JESUS wept his love!
This haunted spot! what shall restrain
  The tears these memories move!
Where two-score Brothers met at night,
  There's solitude and gloom;
Let grief its sacred train invite
  To this old haunted room.

The Duelist.

A brother, known and beloved for his Masonic and general worth,
and had in fraternal contemplation for the highest honors of the Craft,
was killed in a duel. His lodge, though warmly solicited, refused to
bury him with Masonic honors, but accompanied his remains to the
grave in citizens' apparel.

Hark, how the air resounds with death!
Lo, to the tomb a Mason comes!
But where is *the badge* the Mason hath—
Type of a life beyond the tombs?
Is there not one in all the band,
Owns him a Brother now!
Speak, ye that weep around the bier,
And say where the honors were his due!

How he was loved these tear-drops show—
How he was honored midst our band;
For he had a heart for every woe,
For each distress a liberal hand.
Bright in the East our rising sun,
Proud viewed we his career;—
But now that to-day his race is run,
We fling no Cassia on his bier.

Whispering low the cause we yield—
History of his unworthy death—
False honor called him to the field
And death the erring Brother met!

146

No dirge from us can o'er him swell,
    No banners round him wave;
    Emblem of faith we dare not strew
    Upon the sad, self-murderer's grave.

Ceases the knell of sorrow now—
    But long will the heavy sigh be drawn;
    Vacant the East! ah, heavy woe!
    Our Wisdom, Strength and Beauty gone.
    But worst the grief this thought will bring
    To our fraternal home—
    Brightest and dearest, thou art passed
    Dishonored to an early tomb!

The Tracing-Board.

The following was composed to be accompanied, in the recitation,
by the emblems respectively named. Twelve of these are selected as
the most significant of the furniture and jewels of the lodge.

Tools and implements of Architecture are selected to imprint on
the memory wise and serious truths.

A bundle of Maxims, quaint, ancient and true,
A Code of good morals for me, Sirs, and you,
To warn us and guide us in what we shall do.

The SQUARE is Morality, just and benign—
The LEVEL, Equality, nature's design—
The PLUMB, it is Rectitude speaks in that line.

The swift flight of Time, by the HOUR-GLASS shown,
The GAUGE so distributes that each hath its own—
The COMPASS restricts us to Prudence alone.

The TROWEL is Peace, of all lessons the best—
The GAVEL, excrescences helps to divest—
The SHEAF, Masons' wages assures us and rest.

The CABLE-TOW speaks of a COVENANT sure—
The APRON sweet innocence, lamb-like and pure—
The DAGGER of what the true heart will endure.

What riches of wisdom and treasures of bliss!
Instructed by them none can labor amiss;
If tempted with passion, be cautioned by *this!*

When *discord* appears, spread the Cement of love!
When vice would o'ercome you *this* Monitor prove,
When falling, from *this* learn uprightly to move!

Should death be forgotten, recall the great theme,
For lo, life is passing in this passing stream!
With Fervency toil, ere your wages you claim!

Blest Purity's spirit, celestial and clean
Unsoiled by life's errors, *this* emblem is seen!
With *this* clear the conscience of all that is mean!

One third of the day give to Mercy and Prayer!
Remember the Covenant's registered *there!*
Let *this* speak of Judgment and traitors, beware!

A bundle of Maxims, quaint, ancient and true,
A Code of good morals for me, Sirs, and you,
To warn us and guide us in what we shall do.

Fellow Crafts' Song.

Founded upon the scriptural passage appropriate to this Degree,
viz., Amos vii, 7, 8.

His laws inspire our being—
Our light is from His sun;
Beneath the EYE ALL-SEEING,
Our Mason's work is done:
His Plumb-line in uprightness
Our faithful guide shall be;
And in the SOURCE of BRIGHTNESS
Our willing eyes shall see.

THOU, FATHER, art the Giver
To every earnest prayer!
O, be the GUIDE forever
To this, our Brother dear!
By law and precept holy,
By token, word, and sign,
Exalt him, now so lowly,
Upon this GRAND DESIGN.

Within thy Chamber name him
 A WORKMAN, wise and true!
While loving Crafts shall claim him
 In bonds of friendship due:
Thus shall these walls extol THEE
 And future ages prove
What Masons ever call THEE,
 THE GOD OF TRUTH AND LOVE!

The Teacher to His Pupils.

The first session of the NATIONAL MASONIC SCHOOL OF INSTRUCTION, at Louisville, Kentucky, May, 1859, was a scene of great interest to the participants. The assemblage was large and enthusiastic, representing many portions of the country. As a Farewell, the writer made the following his Valedictory as President of the School:

From the hills of old Virginia, from the meadows fat and rare,
From the banks of broad Ohio, and of others broad and fair,—
From the borders of our neighboring States, true neighbors each
 they stand,
You have come responsive, Brothers, and have gripped me by
 the hand.

You have brought me words of greeting,—words I never can
 forget;—
Have given me light my eyes will see till life's poor sun has
 set;—
You have told with signs significant, your messages so true,
And now, at parting, one kind word I offer, Friends, to you.

A goodly group around us! the thoughtful air of Greene—
The cheerful gaze of Webster,—and Williams' modest mien,—
The chivalry of Bullock, that courteous look and bow,—
The sterling sense, the honest voice, the gentleness of Howe.

These are the types of all who've sat unwearied 'neath the voice
That told of Masons' labors and of Masons' well-earned joys;
Deep in the souls of these have sunk th' unchangeable and true,
The mighty COVENANTS that bind, dear Brothers, me and you.

Here too, those welcomed lights have shone, ay, welcome as the
sun,
Whose fame as skillful builders has in distant lands been won—
The veterans Penn and Norris, Tracey, vigilant and leal,
And Hunt, the genial-hearted, and Bayless, true as steel.

To all who *work* as these work, to all who *love* like them,
To all who *build* as they build the NEW JERUSALEM,
Be *wages* such as they shall have, when standing in the West
They hear the Master call them, "Come, ye faithful, to your
rest."

True, zealous, loving men! on this tempestuous, rocky shore
I may not meet—ah sad to think—not meet or greet you more;
Each day speaks louder in my ears the uncertainties of time,
And death amidst life's music louder peals his solemn chime.

Then each FAREWELL! bear homeward LIGHT our fathers well
approved,
Set up the Pillars, rear the Walls;—'twas work our fathers loved:
Time will your fond devotion to unending ages tell;
God will o'ersee and bless you! Brothers, faithfully, farewell!

Tribute to a Friend.

Dear Brother, 'tis no light design,
Inspires this desultory line—
When gratitude and love combine
  There's surely something in it!
My thoughts involuntary flow
To that bright season spent with you;
A tribute to the same is due
  And now I will begin it.

If I should change my homestead place
From Old Kentucky turn my face,
I do with truthfulness confess
  An Alabama notion:
Such ardor in our noble cause,—
Such knowledge of our ancient laws—
The very memory of it draws
  My soul with strong emotion.

And you with ripest wisdom fraught
You, mild, experienced, firm—who've brought
The hearts of all to love, and taught
  Them Wisdom, Strength, and Beauty—
Of all the thousands whom I know
Co-laborers on the Mountain's brow,
Around our mystic Temple, few
  Perform like you their duty!

152

Clopton and Wood:—God bless the twain!
There's hope while such as they remain,
Whose every thought and word is gain
   To the old Craft that love them!
Far hence their final summons be—
May children's children crown their knee,
And grateful tears bedew the tree
   That's set at last above them!

The Two Visits.

I saw him *first* one snowy winter night—
  But summer's fire glowed in his youthful breast—
A humble seeker for Masonic light,
  A pilgrim journeying for Masonic rest:
From the bright orient southward to the west
  Darkly he journeyed, while our eyes inquired
If form, and heart, and garb fulfilled our test?
  From the ordeal he came, as one inspired,
  And glad amongst us stood, enlightened and attired.

Once more I saw him—but his eyes were hid,
  Hoodwinked by death; as with an iron band
His limbs were fettered; 'neath the coffin-lid
  The strong man lay extended, and his hand
Whose grip had thrilled me, ah! how dead it spanned

His pulseless breast! yet round our brother's head
Thrice we encircled, though with grief unmanned,
   And with respectful tenderness we spread
   Upon his breast green sprigs, fit presents to the dead.

For he had journeyed further, learned a lore
   Profounder, drank in purer light than we,
And of desired treasure gathered more
   Than dwells in all the mines of Masonry!
What unto us is veiled in mystery
   Was real to him, and by his Master's side,
Knowing as he was known, *the dead was free!*
   Therefore we paid our homage to the dead,
   And "we shall meet again our Brother dear" we said.

And we *shall* meet again, not as in quest
   Of light Masonic, nor as in that time
When last I saw him pallid in his rest,
   But in a Lodge transcendently sublime!
Death there shall ring no funeral chime—
   No weeping band shall go about its dead,—
But light and life inspire an endless hymn:
   Ah happy we whose very grave may shed
   Effulgent hope and joy as round its brink we tread!

Brother's Last Request.

A Freemason dying, sent a message to the writer, asking him to come and pronounce the Masonic Eulogy over his remains. But the distance was too great and the message too long delayed.

How tender must the love of Masons be
When in the dying moment they can think
Of one another! few the human ties
That are not severed by the approach of death!
He quenches common friendships! blunts the edge
Of mere acquaintance! rends the cable-tow
Of social ties or scatters them like chaff!
But on the love of Masons—golden chain,
Stronger than iron—death can lay no hand!
Powerless, conquered, stingless, hateful death!

Brother! when struggling thus in the last fight—
That fight I too must struggle in and soon—
Did you remember me? did the bright hours
We sat together midst the Sons of Light
Come o'er your spirit like a happy dream?
Did you recall the Mason-songs we sung?
Or what in sweet Companionship was told
Of gentle Ruth and loving Martha pure
While from the sisters round came answering tears?

Those scenes delightful I can ne'er forget !
Would I had seen you in the conquering hour
That I, too, might prepare for victory !
If the blest spirits of the just return
To this cold world, if Mason-love hath power
To call one visitor from brighter scenes,
May I have grace with God to see again,
 When I shall die, those whom I loved below !
To tell me how they won the victory
And what the joys that wait me in the skies !

A Festibal Ode.

Hark, from the lofty dome,
Hark, from the Mason's home
 Comes a sweet song :
Words full of mystery,
Virtue and charity,
Tuned unto melody
 Rise from the throng.

Chorus.—Joy, the Masons' year is ended,
 Freres of St. John !
Joy, which every month attended,
Pains with brightest pleasures blended,
 Ended and gone ;
Crafts of the temple, to your altar throng,
Children of light, upraise the festive song.

Come, oh ye newly made,
Late to our altar led,
  Hasten, oh youth;
Gone is the gloomy night,
Sweet is the mystic light,
Broke on the dazzled sight,
  Glowing with truth.

Age, with the locks of snow,
Time's burden bending low,
  Fathers, oh come;
Welcome the veteran here—
With every added year,
Dearer and yet more dear,
  To Masons' home.

Master, your toil is done;
Brethren, the prize is won;
  Hail the new year;
Pledge every soul again,
Strengthen the mystic chain,
Long may the lodge remain
  Without a peer.

Centennial Ode.

How the souls of friends departed
  Brood around this joyful scene !
Tender, brave, and faithful-hearted,
  They have left their memories green.
    Could we view them,
  Smiles upon each faces were seen.

As they scan our gladsome meeting,
  It recalls a thousand joys:
As they list our cheerful greeting,
  'Tis to them a glorious voice:
    'Tis the echo
  Of a hundred years of joys!

One by one those loved ones perished,
  But they left the chain still wound;
Every virtue that they cherished
  Here is found as here *they* found:
    Thus in heaven
  Blessed souls to ours are bound.

So shall we, tho' long departed,
  When a hundred years are sped,
Join the brave and faithful-hearted,
  Who around this lodge shall tread ;
    And our memories
  Shall be cherished here, though dead.

Grave of the Grand Master.

Over the grave of the Hon. Henry Gee, Past Grand Master of
Masons in Florida, is a marble monument of rare beauty and pro-
priety. The writer visited the spot, January 24, 1858. The place of
interment was selected by the deceased; it is in a grove of oaks near
the verge of a hill. The birds sing their sweetest through the Florida
winters, and the evergreens, whose brightness is reflected upon the
marble surface of the monument, give no indications of mortality.

> "May I, when given to dust, be laid
> In the o'erarching oak-trees' shade!
> Not midst the crowded ranks of those
> In life commingled, friends or foes;
> Not 'neath the dust of trampling feet;
> Not where the mourners frequent meet;
> But far from life's poor turmoil, laid
> In the o'erarching oak-trees' shade."

———o———

> 'Tis done; this sweet retired scene
> Is nature's own delightful green;
> No voice but the lamenting dove
> That sighs and murmurs of its love;
> No footsteps but the tender tread
> Of those who loved, who love the dead;
> No passion but the sigh subdued,
> Breathed for the friend who's gone to God.

The pilgrim, dusty from a path,
That circles round the weary earth,
Stands mutely pleased:—'Twas well to place
The MASTER on a couch like this!
The BUILDERS, scattered as they be,
Sleeping on plain, and mount, and sea,
Dispersed until the trumpet's blast—
Few of them have such fitting rest.

How searchingly that awful EYE
Reads the impress of memory!
Death cannot hide a brother dead,
But the OMNISCIENT EYE will read
Each act, each word, each secret thought,
Through a long life conceived or wrought;
Well for the sleeper if his life
Endure a scrutiny so rife!

But thou, oh, MASTER of the craft,
A spotless memory hath left;
The pitying heart, the loving soul,
The liberal hand to crown the whole.
And zeal in toils of mystic plan,
Which honor God and honor man—
These are thy jewels—they will try
The ken of the ALL-SEEING EYE.

Rest peaceful, then, while Nature sighs,
And graces where thy body lies!
Lift high that column many a year,
To call the grateful BUILDERS near!
Wait patient for the mystic call
From out the depths of Heaven's hall;—
"Ye BUILDERS, MEN from many lands,
Come to the house not made with hands!"

Rise Up: He Calleth Thee.

It might have pleased the great Creator of heaven and earth to have made man independent of all other beings; but as dependence is one of the strongest bonds of society, mankind were made dependent on each other for protection and security, as they thereby enjoy better opportunities of fulfilling the duties of reciprocal love and friendship.

He calleth us to words and deeds of love,
    As spring calls forth from wintry crust the flowers;
He breathes within us spirit from above
    As zephyrs breathe within the sunny bowers;
He saith, Arise, shake off the dust and go
    Where duty calls, where sorrow hath its sway;
    He points our feet the proper path, and lo,
He promiseth to be with us, alway!

The Dark Decree.

'Tis done, the dark decree is said,
    That called our friend away;
Submissive bow the sorrowing head,
    And bend the lowly knee;
We will not ask why God has broke
    Our Pillar on its stone,
But humbly yield us to the stroke,
    And say " His will be done."

At last the weary head has sought
    In earth its long repose;
And weeping freres have hither brought
    Their chieftain to his close;
We held his hand, we filled his heart,
    While heart and hand could move,
Nor will we from his grave depart
    But with the rites of love.

This grave shall be a garner, where
    We'll heap our golden corn;
And here, in heart, we'll oft repair,
    To think of him that's gone;
To speak of all he did and said,
    That's wise, and good, and pure,
And covenant o'er the hopeful dead,
    In vows that shall endure.

Oh Brother, bright and loving frere,
   Oh spirit free and pure,
Breathe us one gush of spirit air,
   From off the heavenly shore,
And say, when these hard toils are done,
   And the GRAND MASTER calls,
Is there for every wearied one
   Place in the heavenly halls!

The Pursuit of Franklin.

When Dr. Kane, the Arctic navigator, left New York in search of Sir John Franklin, he set the Masonic Square and Compass in large characters upon his foresail. He visited a lodge in Newfoundland at his brief call there. The flag taken *and left,* by his orders, nearest the North Pole, was the Masonic flag It was an incentive to the zealous search made by our intrepid countrymen, that Franklin was reported to be a Freemason.

The following lines were written in 1853, upon his setting out on the philanthropic errand. It is needless to say, however, that the writer's prediction failed in its fulfillment.

Midst polar snows and solitude,
   Eight weary years the voyager lies,
Ice-bound upon the frozen flood,
   While expectation vanishes;
Ah! many a hopeless tear is shed
For Franklin numbered with the dead!

Midst joys of home, and well-earned fame,
   Young, healthful, honored, there is one
Who pines to win a nobler name,
   And feels his glory but begun ;
His heart is with the voyager lost,
Midst polar solitude and frost.

The voice from off the frozen flood,
   Appeals in trumpet-tones for aid ;
'Tis heard, 'tis answered—swift abroad
   The flag is flung, the sail is spread ;
That sail on whose pure face we see
Thy symbol, honored Masonry !

Away, on glorious errand, now,
   Thou hero of a sense of right !
Success be on thy gallant prow,
   Thou greater than the sons of might !
Thy flag, the banner of the free,
Oh, may it lead to victory !

Is there some chain of sympathy,
   Flung thus across the frozen seas ?
Is there some strange, mysterious tie,
   That joins these daring men ?—there is !
This, honored, healthful, free from want,
Is bound to *that* in COVENANT !

For though these twain have never met,
  Nor pressed the hand, nor joined the heart,
In unison their spirits beat,
  Brothers in the Masonic art;—
One, in the hour of joy and peace—
One, in the hour of deep distress.

And by the SYMBOLS, best of those
  Time-honored on our ancient wall,—
And by the prayer that ceaseless flows,
  Upward from every Mystic Hall—
And by thine own stout heart and hand,
Known, marked, and loved in every land—

Thou shalt succeed—his drooping eye
  Shall catch thy banner, broad and bright—
That symbol he shall yet descry,
  And know a Brother in the sight!
Ah, noble pair! which happier then,
Of those two daring, dauntless men!

Monody to the Hon. P. C. Tucker.

The history of Freemasonry in the United States from 1826 to 1861 bears many traces of the wisdom and zeal of Mr. Tucker, long Grand Master of Masons in Vermont. During the reverses sustained by the Masonic order thirty years since, he was a tower of strength to the desponding in his own State, where antimasonry secured its firmest foothold. His ready pen was ever at the service of the Institution. His decisions upon mooted questions were unexcelled for clearness and soundness. His knowledge of ritualisms gave him a pre-eminence as a *working Mason*, while his genial spirit and manner secured him popularity with all who knew him.

The following Monody forms a part of the "Eulogy" pronounced by the writer in January, 1862, in the presence of the Grand Lodge of Vermont:

Dead ! and where now those earnest loving eyes
    Which kindled in so many eyes the light ?
Have they departed from our earthly skies
    And left no rays to illuminate the night ?

Dead ! and where now that heart of sympathy
    That welled and yearned, and with true love o'erflowed ?
Oh heart of love, is the rich treasure dry ?
    Forever sealed, what once such gifts bestowed ?

Dead ! and where now that gen'rous, nervous hand
    That thrilled each nerve within its generous clasp ?
Will it no more enlink the mystic band,
    Hallowing and strength'ning all within its grasp ?

Heart, eyes and hand, to dust are all consign'd—
  It was his lot, for he was born of earth ;
But the rich treasures of his master-mind
  Abide in Heav'n, for there they had their birth.

Abide in Heav'n ! oh the enkindling trust !
  The record of his deeds remaineth here :
The Acacia blooms beside his silent dust
  To point unerringly to yon bright sphere.

Then, though the SHATTERED COLUMN mark his fate,
  And WEEPING VIRGIN tell th' unfinished FANE,
Not altogether are we desolate,
  For oh, departed friend, we meet again !

Song and Freemasonry.

Addressed to a lady who has written various Masonic productions of merit.

  Rich is song when tuned to passion,
    Love, benevolence, or joy—
  Vast its power, and blest its mission ;—
    Saints in heaven the notes employ ;
  Heaven itself resounds with song,
  Tuned by an unnumbered throng.

But its power is best extended,
   When, to bless the SONS OF TOIL,
Masons' joys with songs are blended,
   Rhyming Corn and Wine, and Oil;
Then it thrills the inner sense,
Driving gloomy shadows hence.

Sister, from your heart are welling,
   Thoughts attuned to sweetest song!
But the sweetest yet are telling
   Of the ancient Mason-throng;
Telling of its TENETS three,
FAITH and HOPE, and CHARITY!

Still to us your muse be given—
   Ours the genial spirit-birth;
Sing the Sabbath-rest of Heaven,
   Sing the six days' toil of earth,
Festive joys, and sacred grief,
Love fraternal, truth, relief.

Then, when death his object gaining,
   Stills the answer of your lyre,
These the gems of song remaining,
   Other genius shall inspire,
And the Craft, in deathless lays,
Shall embalm their Poet's praise.

The Funeral Sound.

Wreathe the mourning badge around—
Once again that funeral sound!
From his friends and from his home;
Bear him, Brothers, to the tomb!

While *they* journey weeping, slow,
Silent, thoughtful let *us* go;
Silent—life to him is sealed;
Thoughtful—death's to him revealed.

How his life-path has been trod,
Brothers we will leave to God;
Friendship's mantle, trusting faith,
Lends a fragrance, even to death.

Here, amidst the things that sleep,
Lay him down—his rest is deep:
Death has triumphed—loving hands
Cannot raise him from his bands.

But the Emblems that we shower,
Tell us there's a mightier power;
O'er the strength of death and hell,
JUDAH'S LION SHALL PREVAIL!

Dust to dust, the dark decree—
Soul to God, the soul is free !
Leave him with the lowly lain—
Brother, we shall meet again !

Crypt in the Corner-Stone.

It is a legend in Masonry that the Corner-stone of Solomon's Temple, sunk firmly in the northeast corner of the holy Mount, contains many objects strange and curious.   Among them is a collection of all the vices and passions that were found in the hearts of the Temple-builders when they came up from Phenicia to undertake the work. These, King Solomon was enabled, by his wisdom, to detect, and by his Power, to withdraw from their working-places, and to confine them securely as already stated.

Since that period, whenever a Mason-brother exhibits any passion or impropriety forbidden by his Covenants, he may correctly be charged with having "robbed the corner-stone of King Solomon's Temple !"

Build up, ye Crafts, the Sacred Fane—
Raise up its walls as high as heaven—
But *shape your blocks* and lay them there,
    Upon the pattern given.
Our MASTER bade us labor so—
He marked the years, three score and ten,
And gives us many a noontide hour,
    To cheer his toiling men.
We build no walls for time to gnaw,
No halls for men who yield to death ;—
Our *pattern* is the perfect LAW,
    And GOD our service hath !

He reined the passions' evil train;
He quenched the fires within the breast;
He sunk them deep beneath the earth,
    And *there* we bid them rest;
He laid in love the CORNER-STONE,—
A firm unshaken ROCK 'tis found ,
Our fathers built on this alone,
    For this is holy ground!
We build no walls for time to gnaw,
No halls for men who yield to death;—
Our *pattern* is the perfect LAW,
    And GOD our service hath!

Our Future Meeting.

Where types are all fulfilled—
    Where mystic shades are real—
Where aching hands and hearts are stilled,
    And death has set his seal—
In that bright land called *heaven*,
    Dear Friend, we'll meet once more!
The token in thy parting given,
    Points to *a heavenly shore.*

'Tis *this*, our signs have taught—
    Our symbols old and true;
'Tis *this* upon our work is wrought,
    Which every frere can view;

From the first line we traced,
  On the foundation walls,
To that *bright stone*, the last, the best,
  The glory of our halls.

Oh, what a land of joy,
  Hast thou beheld, my Friend!
Oh, what ineffable employ
  Thy faithful heart has gained!
Thy Brother, weary, worn,
  Longs for the same bright dome,
Where all the week's hard service done,
  He'll have thy welcome home.

Emblems of the Craft.

The following lines were written to be accompanied by appropriate movements which will easily suggest themselves to the enlightened reader :

Who wears THE SQUARE upon his breast,
Does, in the sight of God attest,
  And in the sight of man,
That all his actions do compare
With the DIVINE, th' unerring SQUARE
  That squares great Virtue's plan:
And he erects his Edifice
By *this design*, and *this* and *this!*

Who wears THE LEVEL says that pride
Does not within his soul abide,
   Nor foolish vanity;
That man has but a common doom,
And from the cradle to the tomb
   A common destiny:
That he erects his Edifice
By *this design*, and *this* and *this!*

Who wears THE G; that type divine!
Whose very thought should banish sin,
   Trusts but in God alone;
His FATHER, MAKER, FRIEND, he knows—
He vows, and pays to GOD his vows,
   Before th' Eternal throne:
And he erects his Edifice
By *this design*, and *this* and *this!*

Who wears THE PLUMB, behold how true
And just his steps! and could we view
   The workings of his soul,
Each secret thought, so pure, and good,
By the stern line of RECTITUDE,
   Points truly to that goal:
And he erects his Edifice
By *this design*, and *this* and *this!*

See Wisdom, Strength and Beauty too,
In each design our Fathers drew
    Here on the Tracing-board!
Each has a moral in it given
That tells us of a coming Heaven
    Whose MASTER is the LORD !
Each bids us build ON THIS, ON THIS,   ╱
An everlasting Edifice !

———

Solomon's Midnight Visit.

It is one of the most charming traditions that past generations
have entrusted to the present, this of *King Solomon's Midnight Visit*.
The legend is that the Mighty Sage, weary with protracted waiting
for the Resurrection Day, is permitted an hour each night to roam
over the earth. Naturally looking up Masonic lodges, he hears the
gavel-sounds of those that are working past midnight, enters them,
though invisible, and infuses a spirit of wisdom and love into every
bosom. Thus it has long been observed of the Brethren returning
home at so late an hour, that they are fraught with a peculiarly
brotherly spirit, explained best by this hypothesis of the *Midnight
Visit of King Solomon !*

In a deep, rocky tomb great King Solomon lies,
Sealed up till the judgment from all prying eyes;
The SQUARE on his breast, and his kingly brow Crowned—
His GAVEL and Sceptre with fillettings wound;
At midnight, impatient, his spirit comes forth,
And haunts, for a season, the places of earth.

He flits like a thought, to the chambers of kings,—
To the field where red battle has shaken his wings,—
To the cave where the student his late vigil keeps,—
To the cell where the prisoner hopelessly weeps;
But most, where Freemasons their mystical round
Continue past midnight, King Solomon's found!

Oh, then, when the bell tolls Low XII. do we hear
A rustling, a whispering startle the ear!
A deep solemn murmur—while Crafts stand in awe
At something the eye of a mortal ne'er saw!
We know it, we feel it, we welcome the KING
Whose spirit takes part in the anthems we sing!

And, then, every heart beats responsive and warm—
The ACACIA blooms freshly—we heed not the storm;
Our tapers are starlit, and lo, from above,
There seems as descending the form of a dove!
'Tis the EMBLEM OF PEACE which King Solomon sends,
To model and pattern the work of his friends.

His friends, loving Brothers, as homeward you go,
Bear Peace in your bosoms, let Peace sweetly flow!
In Concord, in Friendship, in Brotherly Love
Be faithful,—no Emblem so true as that dove!
The world will confess then with cheerful accord,
You have met with King Solomon at midnight abroad!

The Spirit of Union.

In the settlement of long-pending difficulties among the Canadian Masons, the writer was called in in July, 1858, with the celebrated Judge Tucker, Grand Master of Vermont, to suggest proper terms of reconciliation. The pleasing task being performed, and the Union complete, the following lines were read at a Banquet that most agreeably terminated the meeting:

There never was occasion, and there never was an hour,
When spirits of Peace on angel-wings so near our heads did soar;
There's no event so glorious on the page of time to appear,
As the union of the Brotherhood, sealed by our coming here.

'Twas in the hearts of many, 'twas in the prayers of some,
That the good old days of Brotherly Love might yet in mercy
come ;
'Twas whispered in our Lodges, in the E. and S. and W.,
That the time was nigh when the plaintive cry our GOD would
hear and bless.

But none believed the moment of fruition was at hand;
How could we deem so rich a cup was waiting our command!
It came like rain in summer-drought, on drooping foliage poured,
And bade us look henceforth for help, in all our cares, to God!

The news has gone already upon every wind of heaven;
The wire, the press, the busy tongue, the intelligence has given;
And every one who heard it and who loves the *Sons of Peace*
Has cried, "Praise GOD, the GOD of Love! may GOD this Union
bless!"

Vermont takes up the story—her "old man eloquent"—
Long be his days among us, on deeds of mercy spent—
He speaks for the Green Mountains, and you heard him say last
    night,
"Bless God that I have lived till now to see this happy sight!"

Kentucky sends you greeting—from her broad and generous
    bound,
Once styled of all the Western wild, "the Dark and Bloody
    Ground."
She cries aloud, "God bless you! Heaven's dews be on you shed,
Who first took care *to be in the right*, then boldly went ahead!"

From yonder constellation, from the Atlantic to the West,
Where the great pines of Oregon rear up their lofty crest,
From the flowery glades of Florida, from Minnesota's plain,
Each voice will say, "Huzza! huzza! this craft is one again!"

Old England soon will hear it; not always will the cry
Of suffering Brothers meet her ear, and she pass coldly by:
There's a chord in British hearts vibrates to every tale of wrong,
And she will send a welcome and a *Brother's hand* ere long.

Then joyful be this meeting, and many more like this,
As year by year shall circle round, and bring you added bliss;
In quarry, hill, and temple, PEACE, nor cruel word nor thought
Disturb the perfect harmony the gracious GOD has wrought.

But while your walls are thus compact, your cement strong and
    good,
Your workmen diligent and just, a mighty Brotherhood,
Remember, Brethren, o'er the earth, and on the raging sea,
How many a heart there is to-night that sighs, "Remember me!"

By the *sign* the world knows nothing of, but to our eyes so
    clear,—
By the *token* known in darkest hour, that tells a brother near—
By the sacred *vow* and *word*, and by "the hieroglyphic bright,"
Remember all, the wide world round, who claim your love to-
    night.

The Orient.

LIGHT from the East, 'tis gilded with hope;
STAR OF OUR FAITH, thy glory is up !
Darkness apace, and watchfulness flee;
Earth, lend thy joys to nature and me.
    See, Brothers, see yon dark shadows flee
    Join in His praise, whose glories we be !
    Now, let these Emblems ages have given,
    Speak to the world, blest SAVIOUR, of thee.

Lo, we have seen, uplifted on high,
STAR IN THE EAST, thy rays from the sky !
Lo, we have heard, what joy to our ear—
Come, ye redeemed, and welcome Him here !

Light to the blind, they've wandered too long—
Feet to the lame, the weak are made strong—
Hope to the joyless, freely 'tis given—
Life to the dead, and *music to heaven!*

Praise to the Lord, keep silence no more!
Ransomed, rejoice from mountain to shore!
Streams in the desert, sing as ye stray!
Sorrow and sadness, vanish away!

The Passage of Time.

Lo, the sands swiftly run! behold our lives
Dropping like foliage to a solemn close!
To-day the bud bright expectation gives—
To-morrow blossoms to a transient rose—
Another morn and its whole beauty goes:
Its leaves are scattered wastefully around,
No heart remembering—another glows
Upon the stem—another hope is crowned;
And this is human life, the life the dead have found.

Count well the moments then; fill up the day;
Brothers, let Wisdom's hand your life-plans trace;
The Temple will be finished, though *we* may
Not see the STONE exalted to its place!
It is enough that God will see and bless!

Labor while it is day! there's work for all
The Trestle-board proclaims it, and, alas!
Too soon will night spread o'er its hueless pall—
Too soon the grave—the grave—from which there's no recall!

Clouds may obscure us; slander may detract—
The foes of truth and rectitude unite—
But while within our Mystic Sphere we act
There lives no power can hinder or affright;
The MASTER's EYE still oversees the right;
Heaven's books record it with angelic pen;
And when death's summons calls us up the height,
A full reward for labor shall we gain,
In God's own Temple, freed from sorrow, toil, and pain.

The Model Mason.

There's a fine, old Mason in the North, he's genial, wise and true,
His list of brothers comprehends, dear Brother, me and you;
So warm's his heart the snow-blast fails to chill his generous
  blood,
And his hand is like a giant's when outstretched to man or
  God;—
Reproach nor blame, nor any shame has checked his course or
  dimmed his fame—
    All honor to his name!

This fine old Mason is but one of a large family;
In every LODGE you'll find his kin, you'll find them two or three;
You'll know them when you see them, for they have their father's face,
A generous knack of speaking truth and doing good always;—
Reproach nor blame, nor any shame, has checked their course or dimmed their fame—
FREEMASONS is their name!

Ah many an orphan smiles upon the kindred as they pass;
And many a widow's prayers confess their sympathizing grace;
The FATHER of this Brotherhood himself doth smile to see
Their works—they're numbered all in heaven those deeds of charity!
Reproach nor blame, nor any shame can check their course or dim their fame,
All honor to their name!

———

The Loving Tie.

The Loving Tie we feel,
No language can reveal—
'Tis seen in the sheen of a fond Brother's eye;
It trembles on the ear
When melting with a tear,
A Brother bids us cease to sigh.

Behold how good and how pleasant
For Brothers in unity to dwell!
As heaven's dews are shed
On Zion's sacred head,
The blessings of the Lord we feel.

'Twas at a sufferer's bed
Now moldering with the dead,
This *Bond*, ah, so fond, was discovered first to me!
I saw his dying eye,
Light up with speechless joy,
And I felt how fond that love must be.

I ever will proclaim
With gratitude the name
Of Him, the DIVINE, who has granted this to me—
That weary tho' I stray
O'er nature's rugged way,
I never, never, alone can be.

There's some I know will smile
And others may revile—
'Tis so as we know with the evil heart alway—
But if I can but prove
Through life *a Mason's love*,
I little care what man may say!

The Hour Glass.

Life's sands are dropping, dropping,—
   Each grain a moment dies:
No stay has time, nor stopping—
   Behold how swift he flies!
He bears away our rarest—
   They smile and disappear;
The cold grave wraps our fairest—
   Each falling grain's a tear.

Life's sands are softly falling,—
   Death's foot is light as snow:
'Tis fearful, 'tis appalling,
   To see how swift they flow;
To read the fatal warning,
   The sands so plainly tell;
To feel there's no returning
   Through death's dark shadowy dale.

Life's sands give admonition,
   To use the moments well;
Each grain bears holy mission,
   And this the tale they tell:—
" Let zeal than time run faster,
   Each grain some good afford,
Then at the last, THE MASTER
   Shall double our reward !"

The Cheerful Hour at High XII.

One hour with you, one hour with you,
　　No doubt, nor care, nor strife,
Is worth a year as ages go,
　　In all that sweetens life.
One hour with *you*, and *you*, and *you*,
　　Bright links in mystic chain—
Oh may we oft these joys renew,
　　And often meet again.

Your eyes with love's own language free,
　　Your hand-grips, strong and true,
Your voice, your heart, do welcome me
　　To spend an hour with you.

I come when morning skies are bright,
　　To work my Mason's due—
To labor is my chief delight,
　　And spend an hour with you.

I go when evening gilds the west,
　　I breathe the fond adieu,
But hope again, by fortune blest,
　　To spend an hour with you.

And if perchance the page is closed
　　On which my life is given,
I would beseech the Masons' GOD
　　That we may meet in HEAVEN!

In HEAVEN with *you*, and *you*, and *you*,
   To join the blissful strain ;
Oh may we *there* these joys renew
   And meet IN HEAVEN again !

———

Knight Templar's Dirge.

Precious in the sight of heaven
   Is the place where Christians die ;
Souls with all their sins forgiven,
   To the courts of glory fly ;
Every sorrow, every burden,
   Every CROSS they lay it down ;
JESUS gives them richest guerdon
   In his own immortal CROWN.

Here, above OUR BROTHER weeping,
   Through our tears we seize this hope—
He in JESUS sweetly sleeping,
   Shall awake in glory up !
He has borne his CROSS in sorrow—
   Weary pilgrim, all forlorn—
When the sun shines bright to-morrow,
   'Twill reveal his sparkling CROWN.

Knights of Christ, your ranks are broken!
   Close your front! the foe is nigh!
Shield to Shield behold the TOKEN
   As he saw it in the sky!
BY THAT SIGN so bright, so glorious,
   YE SHALL CONQUER if ye strive,
And like him, though dead, victorious
   In the courts of JESUS live!

———

The Test.

The expression "I am willing to be tried again," has a highly
important use in the theory of Masonry.

I never have denied—
   I'm willing to be tried—
A call for sympathy from sorrowing man;
   My own hard griefs impel
   My heart for such to feel,
And I am willing to be tried again.

The claim, so often made,
   For shelter and for aid,
I never have refused, and never can:
   And though my purse was scant,
   The poor did never want,
And I am willing to be tried again.

Is counsel craved, I give—
What pleasure to relieve
The doubts my neighbor's spirit that unman!
The wisdom given to me,
To him is offered free,
And I am willing to be tried again.

My brother goes astray—
Ah me, *I know the way*,
The slippery way that lures the thoughtless man!
I run to draw him back—
I point the dangerous track,
And I am willing to be tried again.

I've suffered many a wrong,
From evil hand and tongue—
I've learned forgiveness from no common MAN!
Forgiveness I have shown,
As God to me has done,
And I am willing to be tried again.

Each night on bended knee,
The all-seeing EYE doth see
My body suppliant at a THRONE DIVINE;
And there for brothers' need,
As for my own I plead,
And I am willing to be tried again.

I'm dying fast and soon—
My life has past its noon—
I've had such premonitions as were plain :
My heart was strong in faith
That God would smile in death,
And I am willing to be tried again.

A Dedication.

The author's History of Freemasonry in Kentucky, 1859, was dedicated to the Hon. Henry Wingate, Past Grand Master of Kentucky, in the following lines. That venerable and excellent man died September, 1862.

Type of a generation dropping fast—
Pillar of faultless worth and dignity,
This record of the unreturning past
Is dedicate with loving heart to thee!

Of all the mighty Brotherhood whose toils,
Through three score years perpetuated here,
Built with fond assiduity our walls,
Thy services the Craftsmen most revere.

Long through the desert lead thou safe the way,
We pilgrims following with faithful feet,
A Light by night, unerring Guide by day,
Till on the shores of Canaan we shall meet!

Lines to Lexington Lodge.

This Lodge is No. 310, at Brooklyn, N. Y.

A fire was kindled on the plain
　　Of Lexington that gloweth yet;
Each blood-drop from a patriot's heart
　　A lasting horror did beget,
Of tyrant's chain and despot's rule,
With which our sorrowing world is full.

Here on your altars glows the flame
　　Sacred to Truth and Charity;
Each Craft before the SACRED NAME
　　Bows low in mute sincerity;
And peace hath like a spirit shone
Within the walls of LEXINGTON.

So mote it be till time shall end!
　　May circling ages bless the Band
That build the Mystic Temple here,
　　And round the Mystic Altar stand!
Eternity shall gild the flame
Of LEXINGTON's thrice-honored name!

Walking Together.

In thought, word and deed,
We too are agreed,
From the same FOUNT OF KNOWLEDGE instructed;
And by the same hand
We'll travel or stand,
To the same Goal of triumph conducted.

Through the same open door,
We lame, blind and poor
Undertook the same mystic endeavor;
Through the same grave at last,
When death's trial is past,
We'll share the *forever and ever.*

Our *friends* are the same,
Whatever their name,
Whatever their station or nation;
The same are our *foes,*
Whose malice but shows
Their hearts black with coming damnation.

We too, then, can walk,
Sit, stand, work or talk,
In union make sign or give token,
And while life remains
With its losses and gains
Let's see that the tie be not broken!

190

Exhortation to Charity.

'Tis but an hour—our life is but a span;
No summer rose so frail as dying man;
Did there no memory of *our deeds* survive,
Death were more welcome than the happiest life.

But the true heart shall live in mercy's deed;
The *Record* stands where every eye can read—
Where countless myriads on the judgment-morn
Shall see *each charity* our hands have done.

What wondrous mercy doth THE MASTER give
That the true Workman *in his Work* shall live!
What wondrous power the dark grave defies—
The *Temple* stands although the *Builder* dies!

Bear me in memory then, kind Friends and true
As one who loved the MASTER's cause and you!
Join my poor name with yours in Mystic Chain
Although we may not, cannot meet again!

And when the stroke of Death, long pending, falls,
And I no more shall work on Temple-walls,
Wreathe the ACACIA green about my head
And give one memory to your faithful dead.

The Temple.

A number of years since, the author projected a poem which, under the title, "The Nails of the Temple," should designate the names and services of those great men of the past and present generations to whose labor and sacrifices the Masonic Institution is chiefly indebted for its present high position in this country. The stanzas following are but the opening of the design which now, it is most likely, will never be resumed.

No human wisdom framed our halls,
No bodily sweat bedews our walls;
The utmost ken of mortal eye
Fails its proportions to espy;
Nor is it for a mortal's ear
Its songs at eve and morn to hear.

Our temple crowns no earthly hill;
The Turk profanes Mount Sion still;
Siloam pours her hallowed stream
For those who spurn the sacred NAME;
Yet fixed on our unshaken base
Is seen our Temple's resting-place.

Unnumbered hearts and hopes prolong
The cadence of our votive song;
The savor of our sacrifice
Ascends and gladdens up the skies,
Where BUILDERS met from many lands
Rear up " the House not made with hands!"

We would record some fitting phrase
Of those sublime, those mystic lays;
Some names of the unnumbered Host
Else 'neath the moss of ages lost;
One episode in all those cares
Whose story marks three thousand years.

AUTHOR OF WISDOM, make us wise
To apprehend these Mysteries!
AUTHOR OF STRENGTH, the power impart
To build and cement from the heart!
AUTHOR OF BEAUTY, lend us grace
The hue to paint, the line to trace!

   The stones of the foundation
     In the Holy Mountain lie,
   Brought from the sacred quarries
     By the hand of Deity;
   Each Block "the perfect angle"
     Fulfills and gratifies—
   It rests upon the level
     Acknowledged in the skies.

   Each on its broadside graven
     Displays some mighty name;
   'Tis daily called in Heaven
     That roll of deathless fame;

All ages, lands have yielded
    Their honored names to prop—
A glorious substructure—
    And bear our Temple up.

    In such a sacred place,
    On such a solid base,
Built on the pattern of the PLAN DIVINE,
    With time-defying walls
    With love-o'erflowing halls,
Behold our Temple and come view our Shrine!

    The mind would faint and fail,
    The multitudes to tell,
Of all the Ashlars that are here inwrought;
    They're culled from every clime,
    Through long-revolving time
And each bears token of the MASTER-THOUGHT.

    Each bears the impress of MAN—
    Such was the wondrous PLAN,
Of man in body, mind and heart complete;
    Each fills a stated place
    Of Wisdom, Strength, or Grace
By the GRAND MASTER designate and meet.

The Wise Choice of Solomon.

In Gibeon the LORD appeared to Solomon in a dream by night; and God said, "Ask what I shall give thee."

And Solomon said, "Give thy servant an understanding heart to judge thy people, that I may discern between good and bad."

And God said unto him, "Behold, I have done according to thy words. Lo, I have given thee a wise and discerning heart so that there was none like thee before thee, neither after thee shall any arise like unto thee."—1 Kings, iii., 5–12.

When in the dreams of night he lay,
    Fancy-led through earth and air,
Whispered from the heavenly way,
    The voice of promise met his ear;
Fancy ceased his pulse to thrill—
    Gathered home each earnest thought—
And his very heart was still
    Awhile the gracious words he caught.

"Ask me whatsoe'er thou wilt,
    Fame, or wealth, or royal power—
Ask me, ask me, and thou shalt,
    Such favors have as none before!"
Silence through the midnight air—
    Silence in the thoughtful breast—
What of all that's bright and fair,
    Appeared to youth and hope the best?

'Twas no feeble tongue replied,
    While in awe his pulses stood;—
" Wealth and riches be denied,
    But give me WISDOM, voice of God !
Give me WISDOM in the sight,
    Of the people thou dost know !
Give me OF THYSELF THE LIGHT,
    And all the rest I will forego !"

Thus, oh Lord, in visions fair,
    When we hear thy promise-voice,
Thus like him will we declare,
    That WISDOM is our dearest choice !
Light of heaven ! ah, priceless boon,
    Guiding o'er the troubled way,
What is all an earthly sun,
    To his celestial, chosen ray !

Wisdom hath her dwelling reared *—
    Lo the mystic pillars seven !
Wisdom for her guests hath cared,
    And meat, and bread, and wine hath given;
Turn we not, while round us cry
    Tongues that speak her mystic word;
They that scorn her voice shall die,
    But whoso hear are friends of GOD.

* Proverbs, 9, 1–9.

The Celestial Record.

An English Mason, whose name has never been made public, donated considerable sums of money about the year 1852, and made the Western Grand Lodges his almoners for its disbursement in Masonic charities.

Written in Heaven
What he has given!
Placed on the records in letters of gold;
Read by the spirits,
Judges of merits—
Some day the name to us all will be told.

Meantime let silence,
Free from all violence,
Drop its mute vail o'er the face of the man;
Seek not to show it—
Strive not to know it—
Go and do likewise, ye Brothers, who can.

Blest was the offering;
Voices of suffering
Hushed under sympathy noble as that;
Tear-drops were trailing—
Sighs and bewailing
And tear-drops and sorrow the orphans forget.

England, our Mother,
Toward thee each Brother
Reverently turns at this noble emprise;
"*This* makes the cable
Holy and stable,
Binding our Lodges forever," he cries.

The Perfect Ashlars.

The sunbeams, from the Eastern sky,
Flash from yon blocks, exalted high,
And on their polished fronts proclaim
The framer and the builder's fame.

Glowing beneath the fervid noon,
Yon marble dares the Southern sun,
Yet tells that wall of fervid flame,
The framer and the builder's fame.

The chastened sun, adown the West,
Speaks the same voice and sinks to rest;
No sad defect, no flaw to shame
The framer and the builder's fame.

Beneath the dewy night, the sky
Lights up ten thousand lamps on high;
Ten thousand lamps unite to name
The framer and the builder's fame.

Perfect in line, exact in square,
These ASHLARS of the Craftsmen are,
They will to coming time proclaim
The framer and the builder's fame.

The Last, Last Word.

There is no form of prayer in which so much pathos and affectionate yearnings can be conveyed, as the expression "farewell." The following is accompanied in the recitation with appropriate ceremonies :

The last, last word—oh let it tell,
The very *soul of love*—FARE WELL.
  FARE WELL in heart, in health, in store—
  In going out—in coming in—
  Show us, oh FATHER, all BENIGN !
May man's respect, and woman's smile,
And childhood's prattle to beguile,
  Be *yours*, be *yours* forever more !
By every impulse that can swell
The loving heart, FARE WELL, FARE WELL !

FARE WELL—the lights grow dim—the tear
Lingers and sparkles in the eye ;
"So mote it be" I faintly hear,
Winged on the breath of answering sigh ;

It is the voice of sympathy,
And tells of a FRATERNAL TIE
Once, twice, and thrice about us wound,
When first on Consecrated ground
We walked the dark mysterious round;
By all the secrets it doth tell
Of Bonds and Links, and Love, FARE WELL!

FARE WELL—what other word besides
Conveys the spirit of GOD's Word,
Around, above, beneath whose lids,
We wove the INDISSOLUBLE CORD!
Had I the tongue with power to say
All that the hand expert can tell
Of Signs, and grips, and Mystic way,
I could but say, but say FARE WELL!
I could but say "May God *thus* do
By me should I e'er prove untrue!"
And my choked utterance would prove
How weak are *words* to tell my love.

Then let the *hand* speak what it should
And will to witness noblest things!
The bounding Heart responds and brings
Its godlike powers to compass good;
The answering Heavens admit the plea
And vouch a present DEITY!
Angels my loving wishes swell,
And GOD himself proclaims FARE WELL!

www.ingramcontent.com/pod-product-compliance
Lightning Source LLC
Chambersburg PA
CBHW030834270326
41928CB00007B/1050